# A ROCK
# &
# A HARD
# PLACE

A *Lillenas* DRAMA RESOURCE

# A ROCK & A HARD PLACE

*A Contemporary Play About the Christ,
Viewed Through the Eyes of Simon Peter*

by
Lee Eric Shackleford
and Robert Montgomery

*Lillenas* PUBLISHING COMPANY

KANSAS CITY, MO 64141

PLEASE READ CAREFULLY

This is a royalty play. Permission for amateur performances
of this work is granted upon the payment of a licensing fee
of $25.00 for the first performance and $15.00 for each subsequent performance, whether or not admission is charged.
Please use the form in the back of this book to register your
performance(s) and to submit the payment. You may sup-
ply this information in the form of a letter. Mail to:

> Lillenas Drama Resources
> Permissions Desk
> P.O. Box 419527
> Kansas City, MO 64141

Cover art by Paul Franitza

Printed in the United States of America

# Dedication

This play is,
as it was back in 1988,
for

Grant
Amy
David
Adam
Johnny
Evan
Kelly
LeeAnne
Joanna
Marshall
Andrea
Samantha
Blair
Alan
Chris
Shea
Tim

Todd
but especially for Shane,
also for Ed,
and most of all for Ben

# Contents

# Preface

When Robert and I set out to write a play for our church's youth group, all I had was a title that I thought might in some vague way relate to Simon Peter. When we hustled back to the Gospels for guidance on the relationship between Jesus and Peter, our reading suggested to us that Jesus was passionately devoted to all three members of His "inner circle"—the ubiquitous Peter, James, and John—in spite of their stubborn insistence on arguing with Him and with each other, and their bullheaded resistance to the more dangerous aspects of the Master's teaching. He loved them, not for who they had been but for who they were going to be.

I can't speak for everyone, but I found that notion very reassuring.

And Robert and I still hope that this notion is clear in *A Rock and a Hard Place*. If we seem to be picking on the world's greatest fishermen, it is only in the hope of reminding audiences that they were, after all, mere mortals such as ourselves. And if Jesus could bring together a diverse group of mostly uneducated and generally stubborn people who could barely agree on the simplest issues, and that the result would be the church itself . . . well, what an exciting hope we have in Jesus for our own future!

Some technical points about producing this show are worth mentioning. The script calls for a boat—floating on water. Pursuing a literal interpretation of this direction is impractical for most churches' performance spaces (unless perhaps your sanctuary has a truly enormous baptistery). In the original production we had the upstage center area open, like a giant trap, with the visible parts of the inside of the stage painted black. The boat rested on a simple frame, also painted black, that held it at the same level as the rest of the stage. It worked better than I had expected. The boat appeared to be floating in a void. A mattress between the boat and the frame allowed the actors within to convincingly rock the boat when the weather was supposed to be rough. Our Simon and Josh walked on a piece of 1" x 12" lumber stretched between the main surface of the stage and the boat. This was also painted black, and it effectively disappeared against the darkness of the hole in the stage.

We found the gunshots to be very important. Cap pistols always have that cap pistol sound, and since the Crucifixion in our play takes place at the end of a gun, anything less than the terrifying sound of real gunfire cheapened and diluted the true violence of the Cross. We used a fully licensed handgun (I cannot stress this strongly enough—the owner of the gun should be present whenever the gun is used; it's not, as they say, just a good idea, it's the law) with .25 blanks, which are available in "loud report" and "extraloud report." In our building the "extralouds" sounded like the end of the world, which, we felt, was appropriate. But we also found that our young actors could not resist playing with those guns. They must be reminded that blanks are by no means safe. They simply have the bullets removed; the force of the shell is just the same, and that can be deadly. Tiny shrapnel from blank casings have injured more than one actor on stage. So work out with Josh and your Lackey how to keep the gunfire away from their faces.

One of my favorite contributions of Robert's to this script was the idea of Josh folding Madeline's tax form into an origami dove. This can be a delightful visual image if your Josh has practiced the trick sufficiently. In the back pages of this script I have included directions for one way of making the paper bird. It requires that the paper be precut, but if Madeline hands it to him folded in half, the audience won't be able to tell the difference.

The script seems to call for a huge cast, but we performed it originally with 12 people—lots and lots of doubling. Sometimes the doubling offered fun choices: Babe and Mary should be the same actress, for example, and the Blind Man should be either Lackey or Henchman. This way each character an actor plays makes a comment about the other characters he or she plays.

That's really about all the "tricks" there are. Hopefully the Story of Stories does the rest for you. We pray that we are helping to spread the Truth, and that this play will bless you and everyone who sees it.

And rejoice! Because Jesus has rapped us all on our little, hard heads and loves us still for the people we are about to become.

LEE ERIC SHACKLEFORD
December 1993

**Cast** (doubling possible):

One/Jim

Two/Simon

Three/Mary

Four/Andrew

Five/Kingpin

Six

Teacher/Josh

Player One

Player Two

Jim

John

Mom

Person One

Person Two

Person Three

Person Four

Person Five

Person on Crutches

Toothache

Sheriff

Billy Bob

Madeline

Kingpin

Lackey

Babe

Cherub

Blind Man

Theo

Judith

Henchman

Abraham Lincoln

George Washington

Reporter One

Reporter Two

Reporter Three

Reporter Four

Cameraman

Director

Makeup

Elder

Engineer

First Thief

Second Thief

**Scene:**

The stage is a wide-open space, on which anything can happen. At first glance it could be a playground, a blasted battlefield, or for that matter just a bare stage. Impossible to tell which.

# ACT ONE

## Scene One

*(Lights up. A few at a time, people enter. They talk among their little groups and make use of the space in any way that seems natural to them. They are "hanging out." Among these are two PLAYERS who are playing "scissors-paper-stone." They continue this until the dialogue begins, with no "winner." PLAYERS are situated so that the audience's eye is drawn to them first of anyone. ONE of the older kids finds a book—a tattered black book with gilded edging on the pages. It was once dear to someone, it seems, but has since been lost or forgotten. ONE is fascinated.)*

ONE: Hey. Look at this!

TWO: What is it? Lemme see.

ONE: No. I dunno what it is. Looks old. Could have been lost a million years ago!

THREE: Looks like it was lost yesterday.

TWO: You're crazy. Look at it! It's a fossil. Prob'ly lost . . . I'd say 2 million years.

FOUR *(grabbing):* I want to see it. Let me see.

ONE: No. I found it. I'm reading it!

TWO *(always the boss):* Let me see it. I want to see.

ONE *(dodging them, guarding the book):* No! You'll ruin it . . . it's old! Don't . . .

*(Several other kids get interested now, and it escalates into a mob scene. The book is torn, pages coming out into several people's hands. The action stops . . . there is a profound sense of "now we've done it!" Silence. TEACHER enters. He is the age of the oldest of them, bookish, intelligent-looking. He would be "nerdy" if not for his clear outgoingness. The other guys and girls obviously know and like him; many rush to greet him, forgetting the book at once.)*

FIVE *(jealous, suspicious):* Who's that?

TWO: That's one of our teachers. He's cool.

FIVE: Come on. He's not old enough!

TWO: No, really. (*Just to prove it he approaches* TEACHER.) Hi, Teach.

TEACHER: What's up?

TWO: Ah, you know. The usual.

TEACHER: Yeah. What's all this stuff?

ONE: It was a book I found. It was interesting too. They ripped it up.

TEACHER: You'd be surprised how often this happens. C'mon, let's see if we can put it back together.

FIVE: You know how this book is supposed to go together?

TEACHER: I've got a pretty good idea. Come on.

(TEACHER *holds out his hands and people volunteer pages. The book is almost restored to something like its original form. He reads the pages as they come in.*)

TEACHER: You know what you've got here?

TWO: It's some kind of story.

TEACHER: You can say that again. It's a great story too. I've read it already.

FOUR: Hey, you know what it is? You know who's in it, and . . . ?

THREE: You know how it comes out?

TEACHER: Yeah. I'm surprised you don't know.

TWO: Hey, tell us about it, man!

OTHERS: Yeah! OK, yeah! (*Etc.*)

TEACHER: Got a better idea. We'll act it out. This part begins with a guy named Simon . . .

TWO: Hey! I'll be Simon!

(TEACHER *looks at him.*)

TEACHER: You don't even know who he is or what he does.

TWO: Yeah, but he's in there a lot. I saw his name over and over. That's who I want to be.

TEACHER: O—K. Look, I'll assign the rest of the parts, and I'll tell each of you what to do, OK? It'll be fun. Ummm . . . you (*to* FOUR) will be his brother. Your name is Andrew.

FOUR: Andrew. Got it. What's he like?

TEACHER: I'll tell you as we go along. You . . . (*indicating a girl,* THREE) will be a baaaad woman. Maybe two bad women.

OTHERS: That's perfect. I know that's right *(and so on)*.

THREE *(best news she ever heard)*: All right!

TEACHER: And you . . . *(to* ONE*)* will be a fellow with a loud mouth . . .

OTHERS: Perfect! Couldn't be better! *(And so on)*

TEACHER: . . . But a good man, in a sense. And you . . . *(to* FIVE*)* will be a very, very bad man. In fact, you'll be all the bad men in the world.

*(This time* OTHERS *are quiet. They're glad they didn't get picked for this.* FIVE *is like a statue; he nods "OK.")*

TWO: Who're you gonna be, Teach?

TEACHER: If nobody objects, I'd like to play myself, sort of. I'll be your teacher.

FIVE: Is that in the book?

TEACHER: Most definitely. If nothing else, he knows how the story is supposed to go, and nobody else does.

SIX: What about the rest of us?

FOUR: Yeah!

TEACHER: Don't worry . . . I'll cue you when you come on and tell you what you do. Everybody ready?

*(There are general shouts of agreement; it's the starting pistol of a big race, and they're ready to run . . .)*

TEACHER: Then let's GO!

*(And off they go, running back and forth, mostly to offstage positions. The two kids playing "scissors-paper-stone" decide to finish up this "round" quickly—soon they are in their own spot of light and the stage is almost completely dark, only* TEACHER *has a spot as well.* PLAYER ONE *has "paper";* PLAYER TWO *has "scissors.")*

PLAYER ONE: Paper. Scissors cut paper.

*(They play again. This time* PLAYER ONE *has "paper" and* PLAYER TWO *has "rock.")*

PLAYER TWO: Rock. Paper wraps rock.

*(They play again. This time both have "paper.")*

PLAYER ONE: Paper.

PLAYER TWO: Paper.

*(They look at their hands as if they were reading the "paper." Pause, then look up to* TEACHER*, who is holding his page in exactly the same way.* TEACHER *then looks skyward.)*

15

TEACHER: Paper. Let the words written on this paper become life. Let the life take on meaning. And let the meaning be remembered.

(TEACHER *looks toward the action that is to come and makes a bold gesture in its direction—as if to command it to come into being. The command produces blackout.* PLAYERS *and* TEACHER *exit in darkness.*)

# Scene Two

(*Lights up on* SIMON *sitting in a boat, which appears to be bobbing gently on a lake. The sun beats down on him. He would prefer to be somewhere else. After a long moment . . .*)

SIMON (*to the blazing sun*): Oy vey. (JIM *and* JOHN, *two inseparable brothers, enter on their way to their boat.*) Great. Jim and John. My day is complete.

JOHN: Hot enough for you, Simon?

SIMON: I'll live.

JIM: We have a canopy on our boat. We put it up when the sun's too hot.

SIMON: I'm happy for you about your canopy. And I'm happy for the seagulls, too.

JOHN: The seagulls?

SIMON: I'm happy that they get the target practice.

JIM: You're a vulgar, nasty man, Simon.

SIMON: Spare me.

JOHN: Come on, Jim. We should be among better company. See you later, Simon. Write if you find work.

(SIMON *watches them go.*)

SIMON (*impersonating John*): "Write if you find work." Thank God I don't have to work with those guys.

(SIMON *wipes his face with a cloth, senses something wrong about it, unfolds it. It is a bag with the word "BAIT" painted in large letters. He makes a face, tosses it into the water. Fiddling with his fishing tackle, he grumbles.*)

SIMON: Simon, what did you ever do to deserve this existence, I'd really like to know. . . . (*He has a hook tied onto a line, puts it down on the seat beside him. From astern a net is dragging, tangled. He sees it, moves over to fix it.*) Someday I'll invent a tangle-proof net. . . .

(*As* Simon *struggles with this, his brother* Andrew *appears, carrying more gear and a large poster.*)

ANDREW: How's it going?

SIMON: Just . . . ducky.

ANDREW: I can see you're busy, but I'd like to talk to you for a minute.

SIMON: OK. OK, Andrew, what? What is it this time?

ANDREW (*shows poster*): Did you do this?

(*The poster screams:* "SIMON AND ANDREW JOHNSON—COMMERCIAL FISHING." *Some smaller type, then the bold letters again:* "SCHEDULED RENTALS," *and at the bottom:* "AFFORDABLE QUALITY.")

SIMON: Yes. I'll tell you why . . .

ANDREW: We agreed, no advertising. This is a family business, just a small . . .

SIMON: We're sinking fast! Our business is going under!

ANDREW: We're getting by. We do as well as anyone else.

SIMON: You mean as well as Jim and John! We should do as well as they do! They have purchasers crawling all over them!

ANDREW: Jim and John do have a knack for attracting business.

SIMON: They're a pair of apple-polishers. Fawning over their customers. I can't stand it. This (*indicating the poster*) is honest!

ANDREW: "Honest"? (*Reads*) "Locations in 11 countries. . . . To be featured in an upcoming *Field and Stream* . . ."

SIMON: It could happen! Look, maybe you're satisfied with this, but it's not enough for me, let me tell you. And if you won't take charge and make the changes we need, then move over and let me do the driving.

ANDREW: Simon . . .

SIMON: Somebody's gotta look after the business, since you . . . since my brother turned into a . . . cultie.

ANDREW (*stung*): Simon. It's not a cult.

SIMON: What do you call it? You follow that weirdo around wherever he goes . . .

ANDREW: The Baptizer is not a weirdo.

SIMON: He eats grasshoppers.

ANDREW: Well, OK, but it's still not a cult.

SIMON: I'm sorry, I didn't mean that the way it sounded, I guess. But you haven't been out here very much lately. You're spending all your time chasing preachers in the desert. We're supposed to be catching fish.

ANDREW (trying to be sensible): What can I say? This time I'm the fish. I got caught in the net. The Baptizer says I'm too big to throw back.

SIMON: I can't decide if this preacher pal of yours really knows something or if he's just (taps his forehead) slipped a cog in his engine room.

ANDREW: I'm going to hear him right now. Come on.

SIMON: I have not caught a single fish today, Andy. There's still a long day ahead.

(ANDREW watches his brother fuss with the nets, pretending to be busy. He is obviously worried about SIMON.)

ANDREW: Well, we'll be down on the river.

(He goes. SIMON watches him, shaking his head. Wearily, he sits down hard where he sat before—right on the fishhook.)

SIMON: Fffffish hhhhook! (He goes rigid, and painfully stands again, trying to remove the hook from his rear. He can't see it. He calls for help.) Andrewwwwww! Hellllllp! (Pause) He can't hear me. Story of my life . . . I'm in pain and nobody's around to help me. Gotta do everything myself. (The process of removing the hook is excruciating. Unaware that he is praying, he continues thinking out loud.) O, dear God, please get me out of this. I'll do anything, just let me get back to work and not stand here all day looking like an idiot . . . (Magically the hook comes out, with surprisingly little pain. SIMON is stunned. This never happened before.) It worked. (He looks at the sky.) Never mind, I got it. (He looks at the hook, realizes what he's said, looks up again.) Did You . . . ? Or did it just . . . ? What are You trying to tell me? (He dismisses it.) Simon, Simon, Simon, that is the stupidest thing you ever . . . The heat must be getting to you. Standing out here talking to yourself, and talking to God. Boy. (He looks heavenward again.) Not that there's anything wrong with talking to You, I mean . . . I just never much believed You have much to do with stupid little things like this (holding up the hook). I mean, I figure You have more important things to do with Your time, than . . . well, You know. (He thinks some more; this is getting deep.) But if You care this much about stupid little stuff like this, how much do You care about a whole person's life? Like my brother? Are You leading him in the right direction? Is this madman John the real thing? Some of the things he says are pret-ty strange . . . He must be out of his ever-lovin' mind. (He looks around the lake.) I must be out of MY ever-lovin' mind. (He stares into the distance, down the way ANDREW went.) Prophets and preachers. I'll believe it when I see it.

(SIMON throws the hook out into the water and settles down to watch the nets. Lights fade down on him. Long pause.)

# Scene Three

*(Lights fade up again. SIMON has not moved. He sighs heavily, starts packing things up to end the day. As light expands, it shows TEACHER now JOSH on the bank, watching SIMON.)*

JOSH: Hi, Simon. How are the fish biting?

*(SIMON looks, then turns his back to him.)*

SIMON: OK.

JOSH: Yeah?

SIMON: OK, no. I haven't caught a fish all day. OK?

*(ANDREW appears, apparently having been following JOSH. JOSH stares at SIMON. After a moment SIMON faces JOSH again.)*

SIMON *(angry):* Stop staring at me! What do you want, anyway?

JOSH: Wanna be the most famous fisherman in human history?

SIMON: Uh-huh. You're him, aren't you? That Baptizer fruitcake?

JOSH *(laughing):* No. No, I'm not him.

ANDREW: Simon, this is Josh. He wanted to meet you.

SIMON: Hi. It's been a pleasure. Now go away.

JOSH: Have you tried putting the net on the other side of the boat?

SIMON *(after a moment):* I take it you don't know much about fishing.

ANDREW: Simon . . . just do it.

SIMON: Are you out of your . . .

ANDREW: Try it.

SIMON *(with a sigh):* All right, it's always nice to humor the insane. *(He does it.)* Now, how long am I supposed to . . . *(The boat tips violently to one side. SIMON is almost thrown overboard. He fumbles for the net. He manages to pull it slightly out of the water. He sees that he cannot, and it amazes him.)* How . . . there must be . . . there has to be a thousand fish in there! How did you . . . ? *(The boat tips again. SIMON grabs at the net but it slips over the side. SIMON almost follows it into the water.)* Oh, no! . . .

ANDREW: We needed new nets, anyway.

SIMON *(climbing out of the boat):* How did you do that? Who ARE you?

JOSH: Follow me.

SIMON: Wait. This is the most . . . you some kind of magician, or . . . ? I cannot believe this. *(He gets out of the boat.)* Look, I don't know who you are, or how you did that, but I'm . . . I'm not like my brother, see, I'm a . . . well, I've never had any really strong beliefs, you might say . . . I've always done what I was told, and I have my own ideas about things, but . . . look, I have two friends up the river a ways; could you do that again when they come by?

JOSH: Come on, Simon.

SIMON: No. I think you'd better just move on. Really. Please. I'm not . . . You don't need someone like me, whatever you're gonna do . . . You can't . . .

JOSH: Simon. Shut up, and follow me.

*(No one has ever spoken to SIMON like this before. He is entranced. He looks at the boat, at his brother, and back to JOSH.)*

SIMON: Well, yeah, all right, if you say so. (JOSH *smiles, touches him on the shoulder, very briefly but approvingly, then starts off.)* Wait—where are we going? (JOSH *does not seem to hear.* ANDREW *is following close behind. He speaks to* ANDREW.) Where are we GOING? (ANDREW *shrugs "I don't know" and keeps walking.* SIMON, *alone on stage, stares after them.)* This is nuts. *(But he heads off in pursuit. Lights fade to blackout.)*

# Scene Four

*(Lights up on the interior of* SIMON *and* ANDREW'S *house. There is a woman lying on a sort of bed.)*

SIMON: Mom?

ANDREW: Oh, Mama, you don't look well at all. How do you feel?

MOM: Not well at all. But don't bother with me. Who's your friend? *(Stage whisper to* SIMON) Fine thing, bringing in company when I'm at death's door.

SIMON: I didn't know you were . . .

MOM: Oh, you wouldn't notice such things. *(To* JOSH, *cheery)* Hello there! You must be Josh.

JOSH: Yes, ma'am.

MOM: I'm their mother, at least for the moment. Sorry I can't get you something to eat, but I'm not long for this world . . .

ANDREW: Oh, Mama. You say that every time . . .

MOM: Aren't they lovely boys? Not a mean bone in their bodies. Lazy, maybe, but not mean.

JOSH *(coming closer):* What is it that ails you?

MOM: Well, I have this fever, but don't worry about me. I'll be all right, maybe. God forbid I should leave these boys alone in the world before they're grown. Are you a doctor?

JOSH *(a hand on her forehead):* Yes. I am.

MOM: The son I always wanted . . .

JOSH: You are hot. And you are tired. Heaven make you free of it.

*(Pause. MOM is actually silent for a moment. All is still, then . . .)*

MOM *(suddenly getting up):* You know, I think I will make you some soup or something . . . you all look really pale and thin to me. It's this life we lead, I declare . . .

*(MOM continues to ad-lib as she heads for the kitchen. JOSH follows her, smiling.)*

SIMON: She never just "got over" one of her spells like that. Never.

*(JOSH makes a "nothing to it" gesture. SIMON watches his mother as she rattles on . . .)*

MOM: My late husband, God rest his soul, was not a healthy man, and he passed it on to Andrew there. Simon, he's like me, as hearty as can be, all year round, but when I do get something it simply knocks me flat. I remember one time . . .

*(On and on she goes as the lights slowly fade to blackout.)*

# Scene Five

*(Slowly the lights fade up with a dawning-day look. SIMON, ANDREW, and JOSH are in various places asleep on the floor. SIMON is awakened by noises offstage and goes to investigate. The stage is silent. SIMON returns, his eyes still mostly closed.)*

SIMON *(to people offstage):* All right, just a minute, I'll get him. *(He stops by JOSH. He shakes him gently.)* Teacher, there are a coupla hundred people here to see you.

JOSH *(blinks himself awake):* Oh. That makes sense. OK, send 'em in.

SIMON *(suddenly realizing and wide awake):* A coupla hundred people!

*(This of course wakes ANDREW.)*

ANDREW: What's happening?

SIMON: There's a . . . there are all of these . . . uh . . .

(SIMON *exits. An instant later, a mob of people pour into the house, all talking at once and trying to get* JOSH's *attention.* SIMON *and* ANDREW *are terrified of the crowd surging into the room.*)

PERSON ONE: That's him! He healed the woman of her fever.

PERSON TWO: He's a miracle worker!

PERSON THREE: Can you help me, sir? I'm losing my hearing in this ear.

PERSON FOUR: Help ME! I've got a dreadful disease.

PERSON ONE: Come help my son, he's sick in bed.

PERSON TWO: Help my mother, she's dying!

PERSON FIVE: Help ME! I'm trying to complete my income tax forms.

(*The voices blend into a cacophony of cries for help.* JOSH *tries to hear and understand them all. His gaze falls on* PERSON ON CRUTCHES *in the center of it all.* JOSH *grows still, and the mob follows suit. There is a hush in the room. The crowd draws back to reveal a* PERSON ON CRUTCHES, *wavering under the simple strain of staying erect.* JOSH *almost melts where he stands. He approaches the tragic figure and gently touches one of the crutches. With the most cautious kind of tenderness he takes the crutch away. The poor creature holds frantically to the remaining crutch.* JOSH *extends a hand and soothes* PERSON *with a gentle touch, and carefully takes the other crutch. The* PERSON ON CRUTCHES *does not fall but wavers unsteadily for a moment, then stands. After a pause the person begins to walk. The crowd approves. Some hug* JOSH, *others shake his hand . . . a few just want to touch him. All are happy.*)

SIMON: Awesome!

(ANDREW, *meanwhile, has been looking at the mob outside. He blanches, runs to* JOSH.)

ANDREW: Teacher, there are about 10,000 people coming down the street in front of the house. I suggest a hasty retreat.

JOSH: Time for us to move on anyway. You have, uh, a backdoor?

ANDREW: Right this way.

JOSH: Suggest we use it. Simon, hold them off until we get out, then meet us on the road. OK?

(*Before* SIMON *can answer,* JOSH *and* ANDREW *are gone.* SIMON *faces the mob alone.*)

SIMON: Uh . . . hi. The teacher isn't here. I'm . . . I'm a substitute teacher. (*The* CROWD *hisses.*) Oh, boy.

TOOTHACHE: Can you help me? I have this . . . toothache.

(SIMON *is doubtful. On the other hand . . . it didn't look too hard, what* JOSH *did . . . maybe . . . ?)*

SIMON: Of course. That's no problem at all.

TOOTHACHE: Oh, thank you, sir! I can't tell you how bad this hurts.

SIMON *(hand on the person's jaw):* I command you to be healed. Now.

TOOTHACHE: That's it?

SIMON: Yep. You're healed.

TOOTHACHE: It feels the same.

SIMON: Maybe it takes a while to soak in. Go lie down.

TOOTHACHE: It didn't take a while for the other miracle.

SIMON: Well . . . that was different.

TOOTHACHE: This really hurts. You said you'd cure it.

SIMON: Look, whadaya want, your money back? I said, go lie down.

*(The crowd gets restless. Mercifully,* ANDREW *reappears.)*

ANDREW: Brother? Are you coming?

SIMON: On my way! *(To the crowd)* Sorry, folks, that's all for today. The Master has to . . . uh, preach a sermon in another city. Big problems before small ones, y'know. *(He is backing toward the door.)* I hope you all . . . get well, and find happiness, in, uh, whatever you . . . do . . . uh . . . bye! *(He exits, quickly.)*

(Blackout.)

# Scene Six

*(Lights fade up to show* JOSH, SIMON, *and* ANDREW *walking along.)*

SIMON: Where are we going now?

JOSH: Nowhere.

SIMON: Nowhere?

JOSH: No. We're already here.

*(Lights spread to reveal a boat on the water, with* JIM *and* JOHN *aboard.)*

SIMON: Oh, no. Oh, please, no. (JOSH *looks at him.*) Not Jim and John. No, please, no.

(JIM *and* JOHN *have noticed the trio watching them.* JOHN *stands up in the boat.*)

JOHN: It's him . . . look, it's him!

JOSH: Follow me.

JIM: Your wish is my command, sir! (*He climbs out of the boat to shore as* SIMON *crumbles.*)

SIMON: No, please . . . it's not fair.

(JIM *and* JOHN *are out of the boat now and embracing their new teacher.* ANDREW *watches his brother, wondering if the heat has gotten to him. The new team of five is set upon at once by two men.* BILLY BOB *is dressed in a fine three-piecer and carrying a large book labeled "Holy Bible," and* SHERIFF *wears the traditional hardware of a county sheriff.*)

SHERIFF: Just a minute there; hold on. You this fellow who's goin' round and healin' folks without a license to practice?

SIMON (*throwing himself in their path*): He doesn't have to answer anything without a lawyer.

JOSH (*gently pushing him aside*): Simon. (*To* BILLY BOB *and* SHERIFF) How may I help you, gentlemen?

BILLY BOB: My name is Reverend Billy Bob Campbell, sir, and I want to ask you some questions. Are you who they say you are?

JOSH: That would depend on who they say I am.

BILLY BOB: Hmm. Listen, friend . . . we understand that you have given some people freedom from the prison of their crippled bodies. This is a service. We appreciate it. Now in whose *name* are you doing these things?

JOSH: They are healed by their faith in Almighty God.

BILLY BOB: I see. (*Aside to* SHERIFF) Another one of those. (*To* JOSH) With, eh, what church are you connected, my friend?

JOSH: I am not connected with a church. I just do what God tells me.

SHERIFF and BILLY BOB (*after exchanging a look*): Cultie.

BILLY BOB (*to* JOSH): Now, let me see if I have this right. You been "forgivin' people of their sins," that right?

JOSH: You said it.

BILLY BOB (*swelling up into "Preacher" mode*): Now, I'm afraid you can't go 'round saying that. Last time I checked the Holy Scripture, it said only God can forgive sin. Don't you agree?

JOSH: I do.

BILLY BOB: But you're forgiving people's sins.

JOSH: Yep.

BILLY BOB (*cannot believe* JOSH'*s seeming stupidity*): Where you from, if I may ask?

JOSH: Right around here.

SHERIFF: I thought I knew you from somewhere! You're Joseph's boy, ain't you? (*To* BILLY BOB) He used to work in that shop; they made furniture, cabinets and stuff. (*To* JOSH) Mighty fine work too.

JOSH: Why, thank you.

(BILLY BOB *looks at* SHERIFF *with a "Whose side are you on?" expression.*)

BILLY BOB (*to* SHERIFF, *mocking him*): Nice furniture? (*To* JOSH, *dangerously*) Then you oughta go back to it. You'll find yourself in a lot of trouble if you go 'round claiming to be God. It's just not wise in these parts. I'd hate to have to see the sheriff sending out a check on your folk's income tax for, say, the last 10 years or so . . .

SIMON: That's not legal! I know a few things about the law, and . . .

JOSH: Hush. (*To* BILLY BOB) It always comes back to economics with you, doesn't it?

SHERIFF: It's just a friendly warning, you understand. Folks around here are mighty touchy about their religion, y'know. There's some who are real nuts on the subject. You wouldn't believe what some of these . . . (BILLY BOB *gives him a withering look.*) Ahem. I'm just telling you. If you wanna say you're forgiving people of their sins, well, you better be prepared to prove it. Healings are one thing . . . in fact, I have a trick hip joint that I'd like patched up some day, myself. But this other, now . . .

JOSH: Are you telling me it's easier for you to accept a miracle of healing than the gift of freedom to change your life?

BILLY BOB: That is entirely beside the point.

JOSH: Whatever. (*To* SHERIFF) This the hip joint here?

SHERIFF: That's the one. Got a bullet in it, and it's never been quite right since . . . (*he walks a bit, turns*) . . . not until now! Holy smoke. It's perfect. You did it!

BILLY BOB (*not impressed*): I suppose you claim this makes him free of his sins?

JOSH: His faith has made him whole.

BILLY BOB: But you claim to have that power nonetheless?

(JOSH *gestures at the* SHERIFF *with a "see for yourself" expression.* SHERIFF *is happily experimenting with his new hip.*)

JOHN: He can do anything, sir. Anything at all. It'll be a lot easier if you just accept that. We have.

(BILLY BOB *is not happy. He stiffens, prepares to exit.*)

BILLY BOB: We will meet again. Believe me.

JOSH: We certainly will. Believe *me.*

BILLY BOB (*to* SHERIFF): Come on.

(BILLY BOB *and* SHERIFF *exit, with* SHERIFF *waving happily at* JOSH *as they go.*)

SIMON: I'm afraid I didn't follow much of that.

JOHN: You never really were the bright one, Simon.

ANDREW: Now, you gotta admit, it is kinda confusing. Teacher, I'd be a lot more comfortable if we knew some long-range plans.

JIM: I'll go along with that. Just tell us what your ultimate goal is.

JOSH: We're starting a new country.

(*All four followers are knocked speechless by this revelation. Naturally it is* SIMON *who recovers first.*)

SIMON: Now that's what I call an ultimate goal.

JIM: And . . . Josh, Teacher . . . Master! . . . you'll be the president. Leader of the new nation. The . . . the KING! Radical!

ANDREW: I . . . I can't believe it.

JOHN: And we were in on it from the very start. Wow.

JIM: Cabinet posts . . .

ANDREW: Armies, navies . . .

SIMON: We'll take over the . . . WORLD!

(JOSH *looks around at their faces. He laughs.*)

JOSH: Not one of you has the slightest idea what I'm talking about.

SIMON: What's to understand?

(MADELINE, *a young woman, enters, very smart looking with business suit and black valise. She approaches* JOSH *fearlessly.*)

MADELINE: Ah-ha. Just the gentlemen I'm looking for. I understand you've set yourselves up as a new religious organization. Have you applied for tax exemption?

ANDREW: Oh, she's right, it's a good idea.

JOSH: We have no need to concern ourselves with this.

MADELINE: "No need . . . ?" Look, it's a new age, bucko. You'd better wake up and smell the fax paper. We're Internal Revenue. Don't mess with us. If you don't have the proper forms filled out, don't come crying to us around the middle of April.

JOSH: What's your name?

MADELINE (*going through papers*): Does it matter?

JOSH: To me, yeah.

MADELINE: Here, better fill these out. (*Finally giving in*) Madeline.

JOSH (*taking the offered papers*): Madeline. Pretty name. Do you enjoy what you do?

MADELINE (*stunned, no one has ever asked before*): Uh . . . as a matter of fact, I hate it. And everyone hates me.

JOSH: I don't. Why don't you come with us?

(JOSH *casually begins to fold the paper into dove. See appendix for instructions.*)

MADELINE: What do you guys do, wander around the country selling Bibles? Shouting on street corners? Generally acting like bozos?

JOSH: What makes your life worth living?

MADELINE: I make a hundred thousand dollars a year.

JOSH: Are you happy?

MADELINE: For a hundred thousand dollars a year, I can endure my misery, yeah?

JOSH: That's not an answer.

MADELINE: What are you getting at?

JOSH: Can I give you something?

(MADELINE *stares at* JOSH, *thinking he is crazy. But for some reason she holds out her open palm. He gently places on it the origami dove he has made out of her tax form. Something about it stirs a forgotten chord within her. She holds it as if it were made of glass.*)

MADELINE: It's . . . beautiful. No one's ever given me a present before.

JOSH: Maybe you never held out your hand before.

(JOSH *turns away from her as if to leave.*)

MADELINE: Wait! Where are we going?

JOSH: How badly do you want to know?

(JOSH *smiles and walks away.* MADELINE, *entranced, follows, leaving the valise behind.*)

MADELINE: I must be out of my mind.

JOSH *(stopping):* Hey, c'mon. Not every miracle happens with a bang and a flash.

(JOSH *walks away, and the group moves on.* SIMON *and* ANDREW *are in the rear.*)

SIMON: At last!

ANDREW: What?

SIMON: I wondered when we were gonna get some GIRLS in this little parade.

(*Lights fade out on them as they follow* JOSH *and* MADELINE *off.*)


# Scene Seven


(*Lights up on a small area of the stage where* SIMON *is "bedding down for the night." Once he is still, he speaks.*)

SIMON: OK. Let's see. "Now I lay me down to sleep . . ." Ah, that's kid stuff. So, God. Ahem. We've, uh, we've come a long way in a short time, huh? Bet You never saw me as one of the followers of a great man like the Teacher! One question, though, OK? Um . . . *Who is he?* A prophet, a miracle man . . . or, uh . . . (*He looks carefully around himself*) . . . You know, the One . . . we've been waiting for? No, no, strike that. Forget I said that. He wouldn't be like this. (*Pause*) Our preacher always said He'd come with trumpets blowing and an army behind Him, and all that. But he says we're gonna start a new country. So is he just plain crazy, or what? Can it really be done? Where will it be? Who all will be allowed in? Will I be, like, a general in the army? That's what I'd like to be. Yeah. Well, I guess You know best. But I wish I understood this guy better. It all seems pretty weird . . .

(SIMON *stares into the darkness, and the lights fade to blackout.*)


# Scene Eight


(*Lights up on a different area of the stage. The mood is dark, dangerous. Behind a desk sits the most powerful man in the underworld,* KINGPIN. *One of his* LACKEYS *makes a report. An overly made-up girl sits at the desk—*BABE. *She is bored with the whole thing.)*

KINGPIN: You have him?

LACKEY: Sure. We put him in the cellar. What do you want me to do with him now?

KINGPIN: I haven't decided yet. He could yet be of some use to us. These prophets and preachers command a great deal of respect. The people love them. He may be persuaded to help us keep a friendly image in the public eye.

LACKEY: I don't think he'll say anything that don't jibe with his preaching, boss.

KINGPIN: I did not say he would volunteer; I said he could be persuaded.

LACKEY *(grinning):* Oh. Gotcha.

BABE: Who you talkin' about, Kingpin?

KINGPIN: That bizarre evangelist they called the Baptizer. He has insulted me once too often.

BABE: The Baptizer . . . !

LACKEY: He ain't talking so much now.

KINGPIN *(for her benefit):* I have not yet decided what to do with him.

BABE: Kill him.

KINGPIN: Probably. When the time is right.

BABE: No, I mean it. I saw him once. He made a fool out of me in front of everybody. Called me a sinner. Kill him, Kingsie. Kill him for me.

KINGPIN *(condescending):* Sweetheart . . . lover . . . we don't deal with our enemies carelessly, not if we are to maintain control. I didn't come to control the underworld in this country, didn't come to be the Kingpin, by being frivolous. We will wait.

BABE: Ah, Kingpin, you're just chicken.

KINGPIN: Chi . . . ! I ought to . . . *(To* LACKEY*)* Why don't you keep an eye on our "guest"?

LACKEY: Right.

*(He goes.* KINGPIN *drops his facade of courtesy. He backhands* BABE, *hard enough to knock her off the desk.)*

KINGPIN: Nobody calls the Kingpin a coward. Not even you. (BABE *starts to cry. Suddenly* KINGPIN *is penitent.*) Oh, Babe, I . . . I'm sorry . . . you know I get like this . . . I didn't mean to hit you so hard. Here . . . *(Gives her his hand-kerchief)* Are you all right? *(He holds her in his arms, rocking her gently, like a baby. He tries to kiss her, but she pulls away.)*

BABE: No! Not this time, Kingpin. I'm getting tired of this.

KINGPIN: But, Babe. I need you. I really do. Let me show you how sorry I am for hitting you . . .

BABE: Oh, no you don't. You've gone too far this time. You've bought me things, you've kept me in rent and furs and . . . but you never give me what I really want. I want to be able to hold my head up. I want some re-spect. And that freak cost me plenty!

KINGPIN: Babe, you're getting worked up over nothing. C'mon, I'll give you anything you want. Anything. Name it.

BABE: Ha! You're getting to the limit of what you can buy.

KINGPIN: Name it. Anything.

BABE: Buy me back my self-respect, Mr. Lord of the Underworld. Bring me the head of that Bible-beater.

KINGPIN: He won't be troubling anyone again. *(He sees it in her eyes.)* You mean . . . literally . . .

BABE: Yeah, "literally!" I want his head! On a plate! (KINGPIN *turns away.*) You re-ally are afraid of him. *(He stands, silent.)* Good-bye. *(She starts for the door.)*

KINGPIN: Wait. *(He picks up a phone.)* This is the Kingpin. *(Listens)* Right. I'm afraid so. Yeah, do it now. And, uh . . . I want his, uh, his head. You heard me!

*(He hangs up, extends a hand to* BABE. *She smiles, takes the hand, and moves into his arms. Fade to blackout.)*

# Scene Nine

*(Lights up on another area of in a very similar "office."* BILLY BOB *enters and ap-proaches the presence of* REV. FARRIS E. CHERUB, *the world's most widely watched tele-vision evangelist.)*

BILLY BOB: Reverend Cherub?

CHERUB: Ah, Billy Bob. What did you find out about them?

BILLY BOB: It's growing bigger and faster than I would have thought. People are saying he's . . . I dunno, one of the ancient prophets come back to life, something like that. It's pretty twisted.

CHERUB: Do you think he could be?

BILLY BOB: You can't be serious.

CHERUB: No, no, I don't mean literally. Don't be ridiculous. I mean, do enough people believe it? How does all of this affect us?

BILLY BOB: He's basically claiming to be the Messiah. Nothing new in that, but with his miracles, or whatever they are, he has a lot of people believing it.

CHERUB: He also seems to have tremendous charisma. People are drawn to him. All the wrong kinds of people, of course.

BILLY BOB: That's right. His "inner circle" is the usual weirdo collections of hookers, dopers, bums, winos . . . the whole nine yards. Worst of all are the few sad, corporate types who've left their jobs to follow him . . . well, it doesn't make him look very good. I figure the whole thing'll blow over and everybody'll just forget it.

CHERUB: Maybe. We can't be too careful these days. Keep an eye on him. I'm writing a sermon for the next broadcast that will put him down pretty heavily. Once members of the broadcast's Faith Family start making their voices heard . . . it'll be pretty much all over for these nomads and their "new country."

BILLY BOB: Kinda sad, though.

CHERUB: How do you mean?

BILLY BOB: These boys and girls, misled from the Truth. Some of them have been good, church-going folks. Pity to see them end up like this.

CHERUB: I know what you mean, brother. The best thing we can do for them is to expose this "Teacher" of theirs for what he is. It will be better for all concerned.

BILLY BOB: Yeah. We're doin' them a favor.

CHERUB: Absolutely.

*(Lights fade out.)*

# Scene Ten

*(Lights come up to show* JOSH, SIMON, ANDREW, JIM, JOHN, *and several others in various places about the stage, all focused on* JOSH. *In the background, the faint sounds of a huge crowd can be heard, like the waves on the shore.)*

JOHN: I don't know what we're going to do.

JIM: I guess we should have seen this coming. Josh will fix it.

ANDREW: Can you, Teacher? Can this problem be solved?

JOSH: I don't even see where there's a problem.

SIMON: You've got to be kidding. There must be 5,000 people down there. They all came out to see you. Now they say they're hungry and we should feed them! Who said we were running a restaurant?

ANDREW: The question is, what do we do?

JOSH: Does anyone have any food at all?

(JIM *and* JOHN *hold up brown paper bags, their names written in Magic Marker across them.*)

JIM: Well, John and I have our lunches still packed, but . . .

JOHN: Not that we don't want to give them away, but . . . 50,000 people . . . we'll have to tell them to take mighty small bites.

JOSH: It will have to do. Start passing those sandwiches around.

SIMON: It's not going to go very far!

(*But* JIM, JOHN, *and* SIMON *exit with the little brown bags. At once* MADELINE *enters from the other side. She is shaken, scared.*)

MADELINE: Teacher. They did it. The Kingpin, he . . . he had John the Baptizer "eliminated."

ANDREW: Oh, no. What a . . . what a waste.

JOSH: It begins.

MADELINE: Sir? I'm sorry, what did you say?

JOSH: I said, "It begins." This is only the first taste of the future. I don't like it.

(SIMON *reenters. He studies* JOSH *with a face that is almost accusing.*)

SIMON (*in shock*): Those little sandwiches are going a looooong way. They seem to be multiplying. Every time someone hands one back, there are two more in his hand. I can't figure it out.

JOHN (*entering*): It makes sense to me. The Teacher has worked another wonder. It's quite wonderful, really. You don't understand because you can't.

SIMON: Whadaya mean, "can't"?

JOHN: Simon . . . face facts. You're a clumsy, bigmouthed fisherman from nowhere. Of course you "can't figure it out."

JOSH: Boys, please. Not one of you understands, not really. I keep trying to explain it to you . . .

SIMON: That's not true! I understand everything you say! For instance, I know we're building an army so we can take over the government and start our own new country!

JOHN: And when you're the president, you'll set us up as the cabinet! And we'll all be high-ranking officials and very, very wealthy.

SIMON: Yeah!

JOHN: So don't tell us *we* don't understand!

ANDREW: Um . . . I think I'll go and help distribute this food.

(ANDREW *goes, quickly.* JOSH *has his face in his hands. A* BLIND MAN *enters, feeling his way with his white cane.*)

MADELINE: Teacher . . .

(JOSH *looks up, sees the* BLIND MAN, *goes to help him.*)

JOSH: Hello? Can I help you find something?

BLIND MAN: Someone. I want the Teacher, the Healer. The one who is forgiving people's sins. (*At the mention of this issue,* SIMON *and* JOHN *"shush" the man.*) It's you, isn't it? I can tell . . . your voice, somehow . . . If you will only say the word, I know I will see again.

JOSH: If you believe it that strongly, then it is true. Your faith has already made you whole.

(*Gently he pulls away the man's dark glasses.* BLIND MAN *shields his eyes from the sun, then slowly lowers his hands.*)

JOHN: He can see!

SIMON: How do you *do* that?

BLIND MAN: I can see everything! You really did it!

JOSH: Oh, blindness is easy to cure. (*He puts an arm around* SIMON.) In most people.

(*He smiles at* SIMON, *whose own smile fades when he realizes he is the butt of the joke.* JOSH *and* MADELINE *lead the once-blind man away, leaving* SIMON *onstage alone with* JOHN. *They survey the crowd.*)

JOHN: Look at them. There are so many . . .

SIMON: And we fed them all.

JOHN: Well, the Master performed the miracle.

SIMON: Yeah, but we handed out the food. The people will never be able to tell the difference.

JOHN: What are you saying?

SIMON: Boy, you can be really stupid sometimes. Look: Just a few weeks ago we were just fishermen! Nothing! Today . . . look at us! We're heroes, man! And once our new country is built . . . wow. We are going to be so rich and so powerful . . . and nobody will ever tell us what to do again. We'll be telling THEM.

JOHN: It boggles the mind.

SIMON: Look at them down there, eating their little sandwiches. They look like ants.

JOHN: If they ever got out of hand, the Master could just wave a hand and send lightning down from the sky—BOOM! We are *set*, man, we are *fixed* for life . . .

(JOHN *puts a comradely arm around* SIMON's *shoulders.* SIMON *looks disapprovingly at the hand on his shoulder.* JOHN *snatches the hand back.* JIM *enters at a run, carrying a large box.*)

JIM: Hey, look at this! They finally came in.

(*He pulls out a T-shirt bearing a logo: "JOSH ON TOUR."*)

SIMON: We're gonna sell these?

JIM: Hey, we gotta make a living out here.

JOHN: I ordered thousands of them, we *better* sell them.

SIMON: So where are ours?

JIM: This is one of ours.

SIMON: Now, wait a minute. Ours should definitely be better . . . I mean, different from the common version. They should be . . . well . . .

JIM: Yeah, I know. Check this out . . .

(JIM *turns shirt around. On the back in huge letters is printed "OFFICIAL STAFF."*)

JOHN: Now you're talkin'.

SIMON: You know, Jim, I hate to admit it, but that's perfect. Is this one mine?

(JIM *tosses it to him.* SIMON *laughs. This is the supreme moment of his life.*)

JOHN: Gentlemen . . . I think we should take a moment and give thanks for this dramatic turn of events in our lives.

JIM: Good thinking, John.

SIMON: Yes, yes, of course.

*(They kneel dramatically, SIMON looking to see if anyone is watching. He realizes he is invisible to the crowd below, moves to a new spot.)*

JOHN: What are you doing?

SIMON: They couldn't see me from down there.

*(JOHN shakes his head. He gestures to JIM.)*

JOHN: Brother?

JIM: Great and Powerful, All-Seeing and All-Knowing Heavenly Father, we kneel before You today, showing our humility and our willingness to serve only You.

SIMON and JOHN: Amen.

JIM: We praise Your mighty name, and thank You for making us the instruments of Your salvation.

SIMON and JOHN: Amen.

JIM: We praise You for the promise You have made of making a new nation of us, just as You promised Abraham. And like Your servants of old, we are prepared to lead Your army into battle against Your enemies, sparing not one of them before our awesome presence.

SIMON and JOHN: Amen!

JIM: Most of all, we pray for Your guidance. We ask You to show us how best to follow You *(pause)*, and that You give us the power to work the miracles that will show the rest of the world that we are mighty . . .

SIMON and JOHN: Amen!

JIM: . . . because You are mighty. *(Pause)* Because it is You who are mighty.

JOHN: Amen.

SIMON: Oh, yeah, Amen.

*(They stand, looking out over the crowd. SIMON sighs.)*

SIMON: It seems almost too good to be true.

JOHN: Funny. That's exactly what I've been thinking. Too good to be true.

JIM: Have some faith, man. I mean . . . what could go wrong?

*(They stare down at the crowd as the lights and the crowd sounds slowly, slowly fade to blackout.)*

# Scene Eleven

*(Lights up on* SIMON, ANDREW, *and* JOHN *in the boat. We hear the wind and see the boat pitch from time to time. The "water" is rough today.)*

SIMON: Five thousand people. Just like that.

ANDREW *(patient):* We know, Simon. We were there, too, y'know.

SIMON: I just can't get over it, though. Incredible. He's done some pretty amazing things, but man! And we were there. Oh, there'll be books written about it, and we'll be there too. *(He shows the type size in the air—a big newspaper headline.)* "Simon and the other followers dispensed the miraculous food with their own hands."

JOHN: Wait a minute, wait a minute. "Simon and the other followers"? We were there as much you, you twerp.

SIMON: I was called first, big-mouth. And have always been a special favorite of the Teacher.

JOHN: Oh, right. So happens he has confided that I was his favorite, smart aleck.

SIMON: He never "confided" that to me. I'd say you dreamed it.

JOHN: Oh, well—

ANDREW *(the adult):* Hey! *Hey!* Settle down, you two. You're rocking the boat.

SIMON: It's the WIND that's rocking the boat, wise guy. We better go back. It's getting worse.

ANDREW: You may be right.

JOHN *(indicating offstage):* Wait a minute! What's that?

SIMON: What's what?

ANDREW: Holy smoke . . .

JOHN: It's a ghost.

SIMON: A ghost, right. No, it's . . . it looks like . . .

*(*JOSH *enters, casually meandering across the surface that we have established as "water" throughout the play.)*

ANDREW: That is not possible.

JOHN: I notice that he's doing it anyway.

SIMON: Teacher! You're walking on the water!

JOSH *(very cool):* Yes, I know. How are the fish biting?

SIMON: Teacher *(pause)*, let me come out there with you.

ANDREW and JOHN: Simon! Sit down!

SIMON *(already halfway out of the boat):* I know I can do it. Just let me come out to you.

JOSH: Very well.

(SIMON *starts out, slowly. He laughs—this is great fun. He gestures to* ANDREW *and* JOHN *as if to say, "Look at what I'm doing!" He is very pleased with himself. The wind sound rises.* SIMON *looks around at the sky and sea. His sunny face falls.)*

SIMON: Man . . . when you look around, the water looks really . . . *deep!*

JOSH: Keep your eyes on me, Simon!

SIMON: Oh, boy. *(He begins to sink—fast.)* Teacher! *Help!*

(JOSH *rushes to him and takes his hand, which is all that is visible of him. Instantly* SIMON *comes back to a standing position on the water.* SIMON, *relieved, clings to* JOSH. *The lights suddenly trim down to the two of them—the rest of the stage goes into darkness.)*

SIMON: I . . . I was doing it and then . . . then I started to drown!

JOSH: That's right.

SIMON: Why did I start to sink like that? I couldn't believe it!

JOSH *(laughing):* You have an amazing gift for answering your own questions. *(SIMON *is suitably shamed. He looks down.)*

JOSH: Simon, who am I?

SIMON *(looking up, confused):* Hmm?

JOSH: Who am I?

SIMON: You mean, who are you to me? Josh, or the Teacher, or my friend, or . . .

JOSH: Simon.

SIMON: Well, what do you mean?

JOSH: Who . . . am . . . I? I think you know.

SIMON: Wow, you're . . . you're serious. OK. I . . . think . . . I think you . . . *(He stops. He realizes the power of what he is about to say, and it staggers him. He takes a breath and plunges in.)* In a sense . . . well, you're like God. In a way, you . . . are God.

JOSH: How do you know?

SIMON: Well, you do all these miracles, and you know the future, and . . .

JOSH: Parlor tricks. Special effects. Anybody can do that.

SIMON: Well . . . *(He doesn't know.)* I don't know.

JOSH: What do you think?

SIMON: Well . . . what everybody's saying, I mean . . . that you're gonna start a new country, and we'll run out the Kingpin and, you know, organized crime, and the old government, the whole country will just fall down, and . . . there'll be peace, and . . . you know.

*(JOSH watches him, thinking.)*

JOSH: Tell you what, Peter. Until you understand, don't talk about this anymore, not to anyone.

SIMON: OK . . . but we *are* gonna take over the country, right? I mean you said . . . *(It hits him.)* You called me "Peter."

JOSH: Yes. Did you hear what I said?

SIMON: Why did you call me "Peter"?

JOSH: Did you?

SIMON: Yes! I'll keep quiet; it'll be our secret. *(Pause)* So, why did you call me . . . ?

*(JOSH sighs, puts an arm around him.)*

JOSH: It will be my name for you. It means "the rock." Do you like it?

SIMON *(thrilled): The Rock?* All right! Unmovable! Unshakable! Your reliable second-in-command, right? "Tough as a rock!" Right?

JOSH: Yes, the tower of faith . . . and why not? Look at how well you understand my mission . . . how quickly you understood how all those people would be fed . . . and how well you walked on the water.

SIMON *(his balloon punctured):* Oh. It's a joke. I get it. Ha, ha. Can I go now?

JOSH *(very serious):* I'm not making fun of you. You will be the rock. If not now, then soon. Now, listen, Peter. This is important. Up to now, everything has been pretty easy.

SIMON: Easy . . . !

JOSH: *Listen!* What happens next will be very difficult. Things will be happening that you never dreamed of. I need people I can depend on. Do you still want to come with me?

SIMON *(even and cool—he means it):* I want to follow you wherever you go.

JOSH: Always be careful what you wish for, Peter. Your wish might come true.

SIMON: You always talk in riddles! That drives me nuts! Look, give me a straight answer for once. I told you who I think *you* are . . . you tell me who you think I am!

JOSH: Peter. How can you ask that? You're our official clumsy, bigmouthed fisherman from nowhere.

SIMON: Good. Fine. Thanks a lot. I thought you said I'd be helping you. That you needed me. You were serious about that, or . . .

JOSH: Oh, yes. More than you can know.

SIMON: Then I'm, like, already the rock, in a way, right? In some way, at least?

(JOSH *smiles. He raps* SIMON *on the head, like knocking on a door.*)

JOSH: Yes, Peter. You are in many ways like a rock.

(SIMON *narrows his eyes suspiciously at* JOSH *as we begin to fade out. Another area fades up. It is the two kids playing "scissors-paper-stone" as at the beginning of the act. They play with no winner or loser for a moment as their light fades out again and the house is in darkness. Fade to black.*)

## END ACT ONE

# ACT TWO

## Scene One

*(Darkness. Lights onstage fade up to reveal a small area—the two players of "scissors-paper-stone." The game goes on until they both come up with "scissors." Another area fades up . . .* SIMON *is sharpening a sword; the "scissors" gesture mirrors the way he holds the sword.)*

PLAYER ONE: Paper.

PLAYER TWO: Scissors. Scissors cut paper.

SIMON *(maniacal):* Cut! Cut, cut, cut.

*(The* PLAYERS' *spot fades.* SIMON *works on his weapon, a mad gleam in his eye. The scrape-scrape-scrape of metal on stone is not unlike fingernails on a chalkboard. He is surrounded by his fellow followers, none of whom are enjoying the noise:* ANDREW, JIM, JOHN, *and* MADELINE. MADELINE *tries to ignore* SIMON. *She is watching for something offstage.)*

MADELINE: They should have been here by now.

JIM: Bet they changed their minds.

JOHN: Chickened out.

MADELINE: No. I don't think so.

*(She waits. Restless, she decides to change her lipstick.* ANDREW *watches as she does this.)*

ANDREW *(trying to be tactful):* I . . . am suddenly reminded of how the Teacher compared us to the flowers in the field, how they don't have to work at being beautiful . . . I wonder . . .

MADELINE: Do me a favor and spare me your opinion. Please.

*(She finishes putting on the lipstick, examines herself in compact mirror.)*

JOHN: Well, what's *your* problem?

MADELINE: I don't feel well, John. Leave me alone.

41

JIM: I've noticed you tend to "not feel well" whenever someone challenges you to leave behind *(takes the compact from her)* the life you once led.

MADELINE: Give it back, Jim. I'm not in the mood to have this discussion with you again.

JIM: All I'm saying is that we all gave up a lot for this new life. It'll be easier for all of us if we make the break completely.

MADELINE: Look, after only a week on the road with you . . . runaways, I had already begun to sell my car, my house, my . . . I don't have to listen to this from a vagrant who never owned anything in his life.

JIM: The boat was mine.

JOHN: The boat was his. He sold it. Well, we sold it. So don't be so smug, honey.

MADELINE: *Smug?* You little . . .

ANDREW: Look, look, look. Let's not fight about it. *(To JIM and JOHN)* Have some patience, guys. It will probably always be a little more difficult for women to let go of their appearance, their possessions . . . they're not so easily . . .

MADELINE *(exploding):* I can't believe you just said that! *(She goes to ANDREW's backpack, pulls out a clipboard.)* What's all this?

ANDREW: These are receipts. You have probably seen receipts before. We've made sacrifices, sure—but they add up to allowable deductions! And don't start telling me there's anything wrong with . . .

MADELINE: I didn't keep records on anything! Do you hear what I'm saying? I deliberately threw away my receipts. I was an auditor, for crying out loud, and I threw away my receipts!

JOHN: Well, there's no reason to get so testy about it.

JIM: You're always picking on him, you know, if you . . .

ANDREW: Now, wait a minute, I . . .

*(And they are all talking at once. Suddenly ANDREW makes a slicing gesture and they all shut up. They turn slowly to face SIMON, still scraping away at the sword. ANDREW goes to him and snatches the whetstone.)*

ANDREW: Will you knock that off!

SIMON: What a grouch.

MADELINE: I'm sorry, guys. I think we're all under a lot of pressure.

JOHN: You're right. It gets to you, sometimes, this not knowing where we'll be next.

ANDREW: Or what we'll eat.

JIM: Or where we'll wind up.

SIMON (*with a long-suffering sigh*): The problem is, you people have not yet learned how to put your faith in the Master, our Teacher.

(*The others give him a slow burn.*)

JIM: Thank you for that insight, Simon.

SIMON: Peter. My name is Peter. I won't tell you again.

JIM: Good.

JOHN: When did this change come about, Simon? You going to change your hair color next?

SIMON: The Teacher changed my name. He said it fits because it means "the rock." (JIM *and* JOHN *burst into a fit of hysterical laughter.* SIMON *holds the sword menacingly.*) Shut up. I'm warning you.

ANDREW: Seems to me you two were given a nickname, too, weren't you?

(*They instantly shut up.*)

JIM: Yeah.

SIMON: Really? What?

JOHN: Oh . . .

MADELINE: Yeah, right after they told Josh people who don't listen to him ought to have lightning and fire rained down on their heads.

ANDREW: Tell him.

JOHN: He called us "The Fire-and-Brimstone Boys."

(*Now it is* SIMON *who collapses into a fit of hysterical laughter.* JIM *and* JOHN *move toward him with the intention of beating the stuffings out of him, but* MADELINE *and* ANDREW *hold them back.* MADELINE *sees someone coming.*)

MADELINE: Hey, break it up, here they come. Let's look like we know what we're doing.

(*All gang straightens themselves up as the newcomers enter,* JUDITH *and* THEO, *both overenthusiastic and a little brainless.*)

MADELINE: How do you do?

JUDITH (*way too bubbly*): Terrific, just wonderful. You all are exactly as I expected you to be! I'm so glad to know you.

ANDREW: The Teacher sent you to us?

THEO (*way too enthused*): Yes, praise God, he did, praise God. We heard him speak the other day, praise God, and today we sold everything and . . . well, praise God, here we are.

JUDITH: My mother and father have the police out looking for me. Isn't that exciting?

MADELINE: Uh . . .

THEO: And our local newspaper started a series on "The Danger of Religious Cults," praise God. And they used a picture of the two of us . . .

JIM: . . . Praise God.

THEO: Yeah!

JOHN: We're very glad to have you aboard.

MADELINE: Yes, very.

SIMON: Since no one is going to introduce me, I'll do it myself. I'm Peter. The Teacher's second-in-command . . .

ANDREW: Peter . . .

JOHN: Since when?

JUDITH: Wow! You must feel wonderful. What a task.

JIM: Well, no problem is too tough for Rocky here.

(JOHN *begins wordlessly singing the theme from the "Rocky" movies.* JIM *joins in.* SIMON *hefts his sword. The disciples chase each other.*)

MADELINE (*to* JUDITH *and* THEO): They get like this. Ignore it. They'll stop in a minute.

(*But it goes on as we fade to blackout.*)


# Scene Two


(*Lights fade up on the interior of* CHERUB's *plush office.* BILLY BOB *stands in front of the desk,* CHERUB *sitting behind.*)

CHERUB: The Kingpin? Here?

BILLY BOB: Several of the front-office girls said so, Farris, but Security says it's impossible.

CHERUB: I would not dare say there is anything he cannot do. But why would he . . .

(KINGPIN *enters, with* LACKEY, HENCHMAN, *and entourage.*)

KINGPIN: Reverend Cherub. How good to find you available. I would appreciate a word with you, if I may.

BILLY BOB: You can't just barge in here . . .

(LACKEY *and* HENCHMAN *restrain* BILLY BOB, *cutting him short. He shuts up.*)

KINGPIN (*to* BILLY BOB): As a matter of fact, I have discovered that I can do very nearly whatever I please. And right now I please to speak with this man. (*To* CHERUB) No doubt you have heard of a street preacher they are calling "the Teacher."

CHERUB: I have. His name is Josh something.

KINGPIN: I would be very disappointed to find out you approve of him.

CHERUB: You needn't concern yourself with that. He is an upstart—one of a long chain of "new leaders" who tell the masses what they want to hear, and lead people away from the church, and soon . . .

KINGPIN: Spare me your lecture on morality, Reverend. If I want to hear that junk, I'll turn on the television. Saturday nights, isn't it?

CHERUB (*starting to lose his cool*): Will you kindly state your business?

KINGPIN: Very well. I want this bigmouth out of the way, and I think you're in the best position to do it.

CHERUB: What!

KINGPIN: Maybe you've never doped this out, but my empire is built largely on fear, and this clown is selling a lie to the man on the street . . . a lie that says: "You have nothing to fear but fear itself." I want you to shut him up, Cherub. And right now.

CHERUB: I will not aid you in controlling people by their fears.

KINGPIN: Come now, Cherub. You and I are both in the fear business. We use fear to prevent change. That's how we maintain control. My people use violence to prevent change . . . you threaten people with separation from God to prevent change. It amounts to the same thing. Now this loser, this Josh person—he wants to change things, to change people. He's shaking things up. In my world . . . and in yours too. He calls you a liar, your church a fraud. And many, many people are beginning to listen to him. People who used to listen to you. I'm willing to bet you'd rather have him . . . put out of the way . . . than have a lot of changes go on inside your church. And I'm willing to bet you and your church can get rid of him.

CHERUB: My church is not a tool to be used for your purposes . . .

KINGPIN (*grabs* CHERUB's *lapels*): Everything is a tool, Cherub. Even you. (*He lets him go.*) Especially you.

CHERUB: Get out of my office.

KINGPIN: With pleasure, sir. It has been a joy speaking with you. *(He stops at the door.)* And I trust we won't have to speak again.

*(The goons release* BILLY BOB, *who falls to the floor.* CHERUB *stares after the* KINGPIN *as he exits.)*

BILLY BOB *(picking himself up):* There is a devil in that man. Satan commands him to great evil. I cannot believe he just . . . suggested we should hunt that preacher down like a . . . a wild animal. (CHERUB *does not answer.* BILLY BOB *looks at him.)* Farris?

CHERUB: Billy, we have files on most of our older members. I think there may be some that we know have gone off to chase this wanderer. Get some people to help you; start going through our records.

BILLY BOB: Farris—

CHERUB: And when you find someone we know, look them up. Give them a call and arrange a meeting.

BILLY BOB: What are you planning to do?

CHERUB: Just simple military strategy, my friend. "Know your enemy."

*(*BILLY BOB *slowly goes, lost in thought. As the lights fade out on* CHERUB *we can see he is deep in his own mind as well.)*

# Scene Three

*(In the darkness, gunshots. Then, the mingled voices of several people: "What happened?" "Did you see it!" "They went that way!" and so on. After a moment, the loud wail of a police siren rises and then fades away. Lights come up quickly to show* THEO *and* JUDITH *running onto the stage.* SIMON *and* ANDREW *come on at a run from the other direction. Everyone is out of breath.)*

SIMON: Did you see it?

THEO: We did.

JUDITH: It was terrible. I can't believe it.

ANDREW: What happened? Did they get away?

THEO: As usual.

ANDREW: Blast! I knew it!

SIMON: How much longer will we have to put up with this? Innocent people just gunned down in the street whenever the Kingpin takes a dislike to them.

THEO: It's like he rules the world . . . what can we do?

SIMON: The Teacher will put an end to it. You wait and see.

JUDITH: Yes. I know he will.

THEO: You should have seen it . . . those three people, just shot down like . . . like, I don't know what.

(JUDITH *puts a comforting arm around him.*)

JUDITH: Well, it's all over now.

ANDREW: Yeah, until the next time.

(*Loud voices are heard from both directions offstage. They precede the entrances of* JIM *and* JOHN *from one side, and* JOSH *and* MADELINE *from the other. All are arguing.*)

JIM: There he is! Let's ask him.

JOHN: Master, when you come into power, who will be your second-in-command?

JIM: And your successor, your heir?

MADELINE: That is exactly what we were discussing. This whole operation must be run like a business. I am the only one of you who has the first notion of how to do that. Now, the Teacher feels that . . .

JOSH: Please don't tell people how I feel. You don't know.

JIM: That's telling her. Teacher, my brother and I will share the throne. Equally. Sort of a bargain: twice the value at one cost! John on your left hand, me on the right.

JOHN: Well, more the other way around, actually.

JOSH: You don't know what you're talking about.

SIMON: You morons. What makes you think you stand a chance, even a chance. You should know better by now.

JOHN: Oh, right, I forgot, Simon elected himself king a long time ago.

SIMON: *Peter!*

(*Before he realizes it he has grabbed* JOHN *by the shirtfront.* JOSH *grabs* SIMON's *hand and pries it off of* JOHN.)

MADELINE: Look, I have this all planned. First thing is to publish an authorized biography of the Teacher, once he comes into power.

JOHN: Hey! That was my idea!

MADELINE: Oh, right, John. I suppose an ex-fisherman could write a better account of Josh's life than a college-educated accountant?

JOHN: Try me, sister. I was with him from Day One, and . . .

ANDREW: Let's all quiet down, can we?

*(The suggestion has the reverse effect: Suddenly everyone is talking at once.* THEO *and* JUDITH *watch, aghast. Finally a screamed sentence from* JOSH *shuts them all up. It is the first time they ever heard him raise his voice.)*

JOSH: YOU—DON'T—KNOW—WHAT—YOU'RE—SAYING! *(He points accusingly at* JIM *and* JOHN.) When I come into power, when the future becomes the present, there *will* be two with me, one on each side . . . do NOT beg to be the ones that happens to!

*(Silence. Then.)*

SIMON: O—K.

*(*JOSH *exits.* SIMON *follows, still trying to prove his point.* ANDREW *follows closely, trying to stop* SIMON. *Long pause.)*

THEO: I heard it was a trademark of the Kingpin's.

JUDITH: What is?

THEO: Shooting people in threes like that.

JIM: Hey, there were three, weren't there?

JOHN: That's what I heard. One in the middle and one on each . . .

*(It hits him. They all look at each other with the same question on their faces: Could this be what* JOSH *was talking about? The lights fade out on their worried faces.)*

# Scene Four

*(Lights come up on an area as* SIMON *enters at a run. He is looking for* JOSH.)

SIMON: Teacher? It's Peter! *(Lights come up on another area.* JOSH *stands talking with* ABRAHAM LINCOLN *and* GEORGE WASHINGTON. SIMON *cannot believe his own eyes.)* Unbelievable!

*(*WASHINGTON *and* LINCOLN *look around to see who spoke.* JOSH *gives them an "ignore him" gesture, and they speak further together.* SIMON *watches, transfixed, as the meeting breaks up, with friendly handshakes all around.* WASHINGTON *and* LINCOLN *depart into the shadows.* JOSH *recognizes* SIMON, *comes down to his level.)*

JOSH: Hello, Peter. It's good to see you. I thought you'd fallen asleep . . .

SIMON: Asleep? I just got here. You . . .

JOSH: Oh, yes. Sorry. I'm getting ahead of myself . . .

SIMON: Teacher, you look . . . funny, like you . . . *(He realizes what he was about to say, then says it anyway.)* Hmm. Like you'd just seen a ghost.

JOSH: Hmm. Yes.

SIMON: That was incredible! If I hadn't seen it with my own eyes . . . it really was them, wasn't it?

JOSH *(smiling):* Really, who?

SIMON: Oh, come on! Hey! I know! *(Running up to where they stood)* Let's build three statues! One of Washington, one of Lincoln . . . and one of YOU! With a little witness plate with my name on it, right down there. What a message to the world! Wow! People will . . . what's wrong? *(He is responding to the look* JOSH *is giving him. He returns to* JOSH's *side, where* JOSH *answers by rapping* SIMON *on the forehead.)*

SIMON: Ow.

JOSH: Sorry.

SIMON *(staring at him):* I don't understand you.

JOSH *(with a laugh):* Join the club.

SIMON: I mean, this is starting to get major-league weird now. You're talking with famous dead guys. What were you doing, getting advice on how to run the country? I mean . . .

JOSH: Listen, this is nothing. We're just getting started. It will get weirder, believe me. Are you going to be the Rock or not?

SIMON: I am the Rock. I am.

*(As if that were their cue to enter, a mob of* REPORTERS *rushes on, obviously after* JOSH. JIM *and* JOHN *are in the crowd.)*

REPORTER ONE: There he is!

REPORTER TWO: Isn't that another one of his followers?

REPORTER ONE *(to* CAMERAMAN*):* Get in close, now.

JIM *(to* JOSH*):* They followed us. Hope you don't mind.

JOSH: Do I have a choice?

SIMON: Hey, guys, great! Television! We are cooking with gas now!

REPORTER THREE: Teacher! A question!

REPORTER FOUR: Smile for the front page of the *Daily News!*

JOSH: How can I help you?

REPORTER TWO: Just a few questions, if you don't mind.

JOSH: Not at all.

REPORTER ONE: Did you know that the Reverend Farris E. Cherub has called you a "dangerous religious radical bent on destroying everything the church has worked thousands of years to achieve"?

JOSH: Am I supposed to be surprised by that?

REPORTER THREE: Is it true you are leading a rebellion against the government, and if so, how do you plan to carry it out?

JOSH: Do you know who your government is?

REPORTER FOUR: What are your plans for the immediate future?

JOSH: Does anyone really know where they will be or what they will do tomorrow?

REPORTER ONE: There are some who claim you are . . . the "Son of God." Can you explain that?

JOSH: Can you?

REPORTER TWO: Why do you always answer questions with more questions?

JOSH: Why? Why does the phone always ring when you're in the bathtub?

REPORTER TWO: That's not an answer.

JOSH: That's not a question. Next?

REPORTER TWO: You're not taking this very seriously!

JOSH: You want serious? I'll give you serious. You've asked about policy. Here it is. If you want to follow me, you have to hate your mother and your father.

JOHN: Do what?

JOSH: Let the dead bury their own dead.

JIM: Huh?

JOSH: Take up your cross daily.

SIMON: Cross?

JOSH: If you want to find your life, you first have to lose it. Sell all you have and you'll have everything. If your belief in me is only as big as an ATOM, the results can be as powerful as . . . an atom BOMB.

*(There is a long, stunned silence.)*

REPORTER FOUR: What in the world are you talking about?

SIMON: Nothing in "the world"! His words come from heaven! *(He seems to be expecting a tremendous ovation, which he does not receive. He goes on.)* OK. I think what the Teacher meant by all of that was just that we need to be prepared to, well, rethink our lives and to get ready for the new order when it comes into being. It's a sort of . . . metaphor, isn't that right, Teacher?

JOSH *(after a moment):* No. And before too long, people like the Kingpin *(all gasp)* and Reverend Cherub *(they gasp again)* and like YOU *(he indicates all present, who are silent)* will see to it that I am put to death. I hope that answers all your questions.

REPORTER FOUR: No offense, but I can't say I find your answers very newsworthy.

JOSH: I didn't come here to entertain you.

REPORTER ONE: Why are you here?

REPORTERS: Yeah, good question. *(And so on)*

JOSH: To do away with your old life, and to offer you a new one.

*(*REPORTERS *smirk, make rude noises. They prepare to exit, begin stowing the pads and pens, switching off lights, etc.)*

REPORTER THREE: We don't mean to laugh, sir, but we've heard that one before.

REPORTER FOUR: And we'll hear it again.

JOSH: Yes. You will.

*(As they go,* SIMON, JIM, *and* JOHN *move in closer to* JOSH.*)*

JIM: Teacher . . . don't take this the wrong way, but . . . have you lost your mind?

JOSH: I didn't think you'd understand.

SIMON: Teacher, you named *names!* Those guys and gals were from big papers, important networks. By tonight everybody in the world will know . . . !

JOHN: We're going to get killed. We are dead men.

JOSH: I am going to be the one.

SIMON: Hey, what is this about you dying? Why did you tell them that?

*(*JOSH *stares at him, then speaks to all present.)*

JOSH: We're going into the city.

JIM: What for?

JOSH: I'd like to see this Reverend Cherub's television show . . . in person.

SIMON: I knew it! You're going to debate him—on national television!

JOSH: Not exactly.

*(The lights fade to blackout.)*

# Scene Five

*(Lights rise to show technicians setting up to shoot the "Farris Cherub Old-time Religion Show" on location.* CHERUB *is being dabbed at by a makeup person.* CAMERAMAN *is trying to find places to set up.)*

DIRECTOR: Somebody tell me again why we have to do this show outdoors.

MAKEUP: It's the Fourth of July celebration. The Reverend will preach and it all ends with fireworks!

CAMERAMAN: Fireworks! Nobody told me we were shooting exteriors at night!

DIRECTOR: I got a headache this big *(indicates size).*

BILLY BOB *(entering):* Has anyone seen . . . ? Oh. Reverend . . . Farris. We got trouble.

CHERUB: What is it, Billy? I go on in just a few minutes.

BILLY BOB: What's the worst kind of scandal to a TV ministry?

CHERUB *(understands at once):* No. Who?

BILLY BOB: Your secretary, Mary.

CHERUB: She was seen with someone?

BILLY BOB: Motel, around the corner. They're bringing her here.

CHERUB: Merciful heavens! Well, I want to talk to her.

BILLY BOB: Oh . . . here they come.

*(*MARY *enters, pursued by an* ELDER *of* CHERUB's *Faith Family.* MARY *has obviously dressed in a hurry.)*

CHERUB: Mary. They tell me you have been . . . caught in the arms of another woman's husband. Is this true?

MARY: It is. I don't see how I could deny it.

CHERUB: Mary, Mary, Mary.

ELDER: Reverend, if word gets out that an employee of the show was caught in adultery . . .

BILLY BOB: Our best bet would be to go public now before the press does it for us.

CHERUB: It would help to show that we had no, uh, active part in this sin . . .

ELDER: Reverend! Do it right now! On the show!

BILLY BOB: Farris, uh . . .

CHERUB: You're right. This is serious. Drastic steps must be taken. *(He closes in on* MARY, *who is terrified.)* You have always shown these . . . tendencies, you know. We warned you and warned you . . .

*(There is a hubbub from offstage. The lights flicker.* DIRECTOR *exits, panicked, reenters.)*

CAMERAMAN: Where's my power? What happened to my power?

DIRECTOR: We don't have time for this. *(Pointing offstage)* There!

*(*ENGINEER *brings on* JOSH.*)*

ENGINEER: I caught him playin' with the power switches! He had switched off the main feeds!

DIRECTOR *(to* JOSH*)*: Are you out of your mind? What are you trying to do?

JOSH: I've seen how much money you make this way, Cherub. This was supposed to be an evangelical ministry . . . you and your electronic cronies have turned it into . . . into a den of thieves!

DIRECTOR: Why, you . . .

CHERUB: Now, now, let him alone. I'll accept responsibility for him.

*(The* ENGINEER *releases him.* JOSH *moves toward* CHERUB.*)*

CHERUB: You *must* be the famous Josh, the homeless vagabond I've heard so much about. I had hoped to meet under better circumstances.

JOSH: What's the matter with these circumstances? Your makeup the wrong color?

CHERUB: You have a lot of contempt for us, for a man whose work is, after all, only a pale imitation of what we do here.

JOSH: Ooh, now you're gettin' nasty.

CHERUB: I'll be happy to exchange witticisms with you later. Right now, I have more important problems to deal with.

ELDER: Reverend, make an example of her. Let's go on the air and tell her whole story . . .

DIRECTOR: Ratings will boom, sir. It can't miss. Everybody likes to see somebody else's sins punished.

BILLY BOB: Friends . . . there is no need to destroy this woman's life just because she has sinned . . .

CHERUB: Quiet, Billy. This is bigger than you seem to see. I agree; we will bring her on the air with us. When the world sees her in her guilt, they will know that right has triumphed. It will make a magnificent object lesson.

MARY: No . . . please, please don't make me go out there. Are you crazy? My parents will see. My whole . . . everyone I've ever known watches this show. I'll never work again, never be able to hold my head up . . . You might as well kill me!

ELDER: Don't cry about it now, you tramp. You should have thought of that two hours ago!

DIRECTOR: Five minutes, Reverend.

CHERUB: Come, Mary. Time to face the world.

JOSH: Bra-vo, Reverend Cherub! You have preserved the faith admirably!

CHERUB: You keep quiet.

JOSH: Who better to represent righteousness than the country's most-watched religious figure? Go ahead; take her out there and destroy her. After all, sinners must be condemned.

ELDER: You keep out of this.

JOSH: But the man who leads her out in front of the camera and accuses her on live television should be you, Reverend. The world must be able to see that you have never done anything like what she did. (CHERUB *has her by the arm, is ready to go.*) Never tried to. Never contemplated it. (CHERUB *pauses.*) Never wanted to, even for a moment.

(CHERUB *thinks for a long time. Then, very slowly, he releases his grip on her arm.*)

ENGINEER: Reverend! What are you doing?

JOSH: Surely there is someone here who has never slept with another person's spouse! (*The* ENGINEER *takes* MARY *by the arm.*) And never wanted to.

(*The* ENGINEER *lets her go again.* CHERUB *has moved away.*)

DIRECTOR: Reverend—you're on in one minute! (CHERUB *darts away.*) Wha . . . what are we going to do about the broadcast?

JOSH: Show a rerun.

*(The crew disperses. Soon* JOSH *and* MARY *are alone. She sinks to her knees.* JOSH *extends a hand to her.)*

JOSH: Come on. Take my hand.

MARY: I can't . . . you're so clean and I'm so . . . dirty . . . *(*JOSH *rubs his hands on the ground, dirtying them, then offers her the hand. She smiles at this, takes the hand. He smiles, helps her to her feet.)* I'm really sorry for what I did. I'll never do it again . . .

JOSH: I know. So forget it.

MARY: How . . . ?

JOSH: Know that nobody condemns you now.

MARY: But I was . . . I was caught in the act!

JOSH *(smiles):* Everyone is.

*(She embraces him. At this moment,* SIMON *enters, at a run.)*

SIMON: Boy, I thought I'd never get past Security. *(He sees the woman hugging the Teacher.)* Hey! Get away from the Teacher! You ought to be ashamed of yourself! Get out of here and put on some decent clothes! *(*MARY *looks from him to* JOSH, *who gives her a "don't-mind-him" gesture and sends her on her way. She exits, happy.)* Well, you can't be too careful nowadays.

JOSH: Oh, I know. Lucky for me you came along when you did. *(He raps* SIMON *on the forehead and goes.* SIMON *calls after him.)*

SIMON: Don't mention it. *(Rubbing his head)* I wish he'd stop doing that.

*(Lights fade out fast.)*

# Scene Six

*(*KINGPIN'S *office. Lights fade up as he talks on the telephone.)*

KINGPIN: Listen! My authority in this city is to be unquestioned—do you hear me? *Unquestioned!* I don't care *what* he's telling people. Besides, I thought we had that bum taken care of! What? Well, tell Cherub to get it in gear and find some way to push this creep out of the picture. No, I don't want him run out, I want him *dead.* I know Cherub's dragging his feet. But after that stunt today with his TV show—I believe our Reverend Cherub will have this man in a cage very soon. All we'll have to do then . . . is step in and pick up the pieces.

*(*KINGPIN *laughs as he hangs up the phone. The lights cross-fade to* CHERUB'S *office.)*

# Scene Seven

*(Lights come up on* Cherub, *at his desk.* Billy Bob *stands before the desk, holding a file folder.)*

Cherub: Used to be a member of the Faith Family?

Billy Bob: Heavy contributor. Very zealous. Now definitely in the group closest to this Josh, this "Teacher" of theirs.

Cherub *(taking the folder, dials telephone number from it):* Hmm. Type that usually falls for these fly-by-night preachers. OK. We'll see how this works out.

Billy Bob: Um . . . what are you gonna do?

Cherub *(deadly):* Listen, after our last little encounter . . . I can't afford to lose face with my people like that, not anymore. This is a personal matter between him and me now. *(Into the phone, suddenly very sweet)* Hello? Yes, this is Farris E. Cherub. That's right. No, no problem . . . I was, well, concerned that we hadn't seen you at church in some time. Mm-hm. You are? I see. Well, yes, we've heard a great deal about this man. I imagine you know that I do not feel his call has truly come from the Lord God. No? Well, I've been quite clear about that. You what? *(To* Billy Bob*)* Hasn't been around a television set. *(To the phone)* No, this Josh character is, eh, something of a wolf in sheep's clothing. I'm sorry to disappoint you, but it's very clear once you know all we know about him. We could, uh, all discuss it very rationally, very politely, if we could arrange some mutual meeting place. Do you think you could help us do that? Excellent. I knew you'd be willing to help the church meet its true goals. Now, I'll probably bring a few . . . friends. No, that's all right. Thank *you.* I think we might even be able to . . . reward you for your efforts. No, I insist. All right. We'll see you then. Good-bye.

*(*Cherub *hangs up, contented.* Billy Bob *looks at him, a little green.* Cherub *scowls at him.)*

Cherub: Something on your mind?

Billy Bob *(pained, slowly):* What have we done?

*(They stare at each other as the lights slowly fade to blackout.)*

# Scene Eight

*(Lights come up to show the whole group, sitting in a semicircle outdoors:* Josh, Simon, Jim, John, Andrew, Theo, Judith, Madeline, *and* Mary. *There are props that give the instant impression that this is the Fourth of July. Among these are hot dogs*

*and soft drinks. The group is laughing and talking.* ANDREW *makes himself heard above it all.)*

ANDREW: I'd like to propose a toast. To the Teacher, and his victory over Reverend Cherub!

*(They applaud,* MARY *loudest. They begin calling "Speech! Speech!"* JOSH *stands.)*

JOSH: Today is the day we celebrate the victories of our ancestors . . . the anniversary of the day this nation became free. So I wanted to eat this meal with you, this celebration of freedom. I am going to be free soon, but as this country had to lose a lot of everyone's blood to gain that freedom, so will I. In other words, this is good-bye. *(A stunned chorus of "What?" from the group.* JOSH *waves them down.)* I've tried to warn you of this all along. But yes, the next step in our plan is . . . that I have to die.

SIMON: That's impossible—who could kill you?

JIM: The Kingpin and his men?

JOHN: Let's call down fire and lightning from the sky and blow them all up!

JIM: YEAH!

MADELINE: Will you *stop saying that!*

JOSH: You don't understand! One of you will turn me over to them . . .

*(More cries of protest,* SIMON's *the loudest)*

SIMON: Who? Which one? I'll kill him now. I won't let this happen, I won't! You'll see!

JOSH: Don't be so smart, Simon. You'll be pretending you don't know me before the night is through.

SIMON *(stunned and hurt):* You called me Simon.

JOSH: You've tried to be the Rock, without resting on me . . . you're beginning to see you can't do it by yourself. Three times before the big clock chimes three, and you'll see. You're no rock; just a handful of sand.

SIMON: But . . .

*(*JOSH *grimly holds up three fingers.* SIMON *shuts up. Everyone is quiet.* JOSH *takes a hamburger bun, pulls it into its halves.)*

JOSH: I'd like everyone to eat a bit of this. It's the taste of things to come. *(They begin passing it along.)* Understand that this is my body, that will soon be quite, quite dead. We'll all share in that as we eat together.

*(This they do, somberly, quietly.* JOSH *opens one of the soft drinks.)*

JOSH: And drink a bit of this for the same reasons. Consider it my blood, which I think will be rather easy to see very soon. And you'll share in that too.

*(As the bottle goes around, JOSH does a quiet "good-bye" with each member of the group. He comes to SIMON last.)*

SIMON: You'll see. I'll prove you wrong.

*(JOSH is silent. He holds up the three fingers again. SIMON looks away.)*

JOSH: I'm going to pray . . . alone if I have to. But I would appreciate some of you being nearby.

*(He goes, with JIM, JOHN, and SIMON all close behind, calling after him. One by one, the others go, leaving only THEO behind. He is openly suspicious of all of this, his former enthusiasm clearly destroyed.)*

THEO: This isn't turning out the way I expected.

*(THEO stares off after the departed crowd, then pointedly exits in the opposite direction. Lights fade.)*

# Scene Nine

*(Lights show JOSH, JIM, JOHN, and SIMON on a higher level than before. The latter three are confused, even angry. JOSH tries to calm them.)*

JIM: Why didn't you tell us? How could you let us down like this?

JOHN: And how do you know what will happen? Can we stop it?

JOSH: I have been telling you this all along. It's too late to do anything about it. *(He looks at SIMON, who for once has nothing to say.)* I'm going up here to pray. Will you stay here and keep a lookout?

JOHN: We'll guard you with our lives.

JOSH: That's not what I asked for. Just try to stay awake.

*(He looks significantly at SIMON, then exits.)*

JIM: I cannot believe this.

JOHN: This has got to be another one of his puzzles, his little word games. Or something.

SIMON: I'm not so sure.

JIM: What do you know, anyway?

SIMON: Not much, I guess.

*(This confession of* SIMON's *touches* JIM. JIM *puts an arm around* SIMON. JOHN *holds* SIMON *from the other side.* SIMON *accepts their embrace for the first time. Then they silently separate and move to distant parts of the stage.* SIMON *sits, weary. As his eyelids grow heavy, the lights slowly fade to blackout.)*

# Scene Ten

*(In the darkness)*

JOSH: Peter!

*(The lights bump back up to full.)*

SIMON: What? I'm here! I'm up!

JOSH: Hello, Peter. It's good to see you. I thought you'd fallen asleep . . .

SIMON: Asleep? No! How could you . . . I . . . hey, are you all right?

JOSH: I'm sorry . . . I'm getting ahead of myself . . .

JIM: You don't look well at all.

JOSH: They should be here any second now . . .

JOHN: "They"? "They" who?

JOSH *(indicating offstage):* Them.

*(*LACKEY, HENCHMAN, *and others appear, armed for combat. Among them are the others of* JOSH's *followers.* ANDREW *speaks first.)*

ANDREW: Peter. Come on, let's get out of here . . .

SIMON: Wait a minute, what's going on?

MADELINE: Guys, really, we should leave. No kidding.

ANDREW: They followed us. They don't want us, though. Let's go.

*(*JUDITH *approaches* JOSH. *She bites her lip, embraces* JOSH.)*

JUDITH: I have . . . some friends who want to talk to you. I think we can all reach some kind of . . . agreement. If you'll just listen to them and . . . Well, he says you're really a bad man, and . . . I don't know what to think anymore.

*(She is interrupted by* LACKEY, *leading* KINGPIN's *men. He goes to* JOSH *and pulls him from* JUDITH.)*

LACKEY *(to the others):* That's him. *(The others move in on* JOSH. *To* JUDITH, LACKEY *gives a neatly bound stack of cash.)* Thanks for your help, sweetheart.

JUDITH: What are you going to do? Nobody said anything about all these guns and . . .

LACKEY: Just keep out of this.

JOSH: I had no idea I was so dangerous.

SIMON: Teacher? What's happening?

JOSH: What I told you would happen.

SIMON: *Noooooo!*

*(He dives at the* LACKEY *closest to* JOSH, *fighting impossible odds. Then* JIM, JOHN, MADELINE, MARY, ANDREW, *and* JUDITH *run wildly off in every direction.* JOSH *restrains* SIMON.)

JOSH: You can't fight them this way, you thick-headed . . .

SIMON: Come on, let me go . . .

HENCHMAN *(to* LACKEY): Do we want to pop this one off too? Please, let me . . .

LACKEY: No. Our orders are for just this one. Today, anyway.

HENCHMAN *(to* SIMON): Hear that? Only a matter of time, wise guy.

*(*JOSH *and* SIMON *lock their eyes on each other—the gaze is not broken even by* JOSH's *being dragged away. Finally,* SIMON *is alone onstage, still staring at* JOSH *at he recedes in the distance.* SIMON *is in agony—close to pulling his hair and tearing his clothes.)*

SIMON: No. *(He makes up his mind.)* No!

*(He runs offstage, following* JOSH. *Blackout.)*

# Scene Eleven

*(Two areas of the stage are gradually illuminated at the same time. In one,* SIMON *is trying to see into a window high above his head. Two* REPORTERS *are trying to do the same. In the other area,* JOSH *is being dragged to face the* KINGPIN.)*

SIMON: I guess he's in there now.

REPORTER ONE: You mean the miracle worker? Yeah, I saw him go in.

REPORTER TWO: Right in the church building too. Great irony.

SIMON: What do you mean?

REPORTER TWO: Kingpin's in there. That poor soul will never come out alive.

KINGPIN: So. We meet at last. I confess I'm a great admirer of yours. I believe you've met the other officer in your fan club . . .

(CHERUB *moves cautiously into the light.*)

REPORTER ONE: Say . . . you're one of his Inner Circle, aren't you?

REPORTER TWO: Yeah! I thought I knew your face!

SIMON: You're crazy.

REPORTER TWO: Well, maybe I was wrong. I'd expect his followers to be a little more polite.

*(The* REPORTERS *laugh.* SIMON *searches for the window.)*

CHERUB: You have created quite a stir among my people. I can't allow that. What do you propose we do about it?

(JOSH *is still, silent.*)

KINGPIN: I expected this from you. I am offering you a chance for your life. Don't be stupid! You could work for us . . . for me.

(JOSH *is silent.*)

CHERUB: A fool! A fool.

REPORTER TWO: I know . . . it was the press conference. You were there "interpreting" for him.

REPORTER ONE: That's right! That was it!

SIMON: Oh, I know what you mean . . . no, that guy looks a lot like me, but, no . . . no, I never . . .

REPORTER TWO: Uh-huh, right . . .

CHERUB: Let me read you a quote. I wonder if it is true that you said this: "You churchgoers who listen every Sunday to a half-truth designed to make you comfortable are only lying to yourselves and to each other. Some of you have been waiting for me to come, but not one of you recognized me once I arrived. In fact, 99 percent of you have always been terrified that I would actually show up in your lifetimes." Did you say this?

(JOSH *says nothing.*)

CHERUB: *Did you say this? (Silence.* CHERUB *begins to quake with rage.)* In another day and age you would be burned at the stake for saying things like that!

KINGPIN: My friend speaks of the law. But I want to remind you that in this country, I am the law. I can do with you as I will. What do you think of that?

(JOSH *says nothing.*)

SIMON: I guess I'd better go . . .

REPORTER TWO: Wait a minute! I just realized I have *pictures* from that little shindig!

REPORTER ONE: You do? Lemme see.

REPORTER TWO (*digging them out*): Yes . . . here! And there he is! Look!

(*He shows the photo to* SIMON, *who grabs it and tears it in half.*)

SIMON: *I never even saw the man! All right? I don't even know who he is!*

(*At that instant, the church clock chimes: BONG . . . BONG . . . BONGGGG. For its effect on* SIMON, *the clapper might as well be hitting him on the head. He half runs, half stumbles down to another area. Lights on the* REPORTERS *fade.*)

CHERUB: Killing is wrong, Kingpin. I can't let you murder this man . . . no matter how great an irritation to me he may happen to be.

KINGPIN: But you're, um . . . not exactly going to try to restrain me, are you?

(CHERUB *looks away, ashamed.* LACKEY *pulls* JOSH *away, raises a questioning eyebrow at* KINGPIN. *The* KINGPIN *makes a slow throat-cutting gesture.* LACKEY *grins, pushes* JOSH *out of the light, which quickly fades on* KINGPIN *and* CHERUB.)

# Scene Twelve

SIMON: No. No, no, no, no, no, no . . .

(*Another area of light comes up.* JOSH *is pushed out into the street along with two* THIEVES, *who are pleading pathetically.* LACKEY *and* HENCHMAN *have guns.*)

FIRST THIEF: We were promised! We only stole because *he told us to!* The Kingpin told us we'd be *protected* if we were caught!

SECOND THIEF: He promised!

HENCHMAN: He only promised you wouldn't go to *jail.*

LACKEY: And you won't.

(*Each of them shoots one of the thieves. The "bangs" of the two guns are startlingly loud. The* THIEVES *fall, one on each side of* JOSH. LACKEY *and* HENCHMAN *advance on him, laughing.*)

LACKEY: We're waiting for a miracle, miracle man. Wonder if you can catch a bullet, like Superman?

HENCHMAN: Let's find out.

*(He fires at* JOSH's *leg.* JOSH *cries out, crumbles to the ground, clutching his ankle.* SIMON *reacts as if he himself had been shot.)*

HENCHMAN: Guess not.

LACKEY: I'm disappointed. Maybe it wasn't a fair test. Shot too low for him to catch.

*(He fires higher, at the hand with which* JOSH *is bracing himself against the wall. The bullet strikes* JOSH's *wrist. He cries out again, rolling over on the ground. Again,* SIMON *reacts the same way. From the shadows, a small group of people begins to emerge, made up of disciples and others. They watch timidly.)*

HENCHMAN: He doesn't seem to be catching the bullets so good.

*(He stands on* JOSH's *wrist, aims the gun at the trapped hand.)*

LACKEY: Maybe it's a range problem. *(He fires.* JOSH *writhes, screams.* SIMON *screams with him.)* Guess not.

*(*LACKEY *drags* JOSH *to his feet. Blood streams from* JOSH's *wrists and from the wound in his ankle.* SIMON *struggles to his knees. On the other side of the stage, a group of people appears. They watch.)*

JIM: Somebody ought to do something.

THEO: Like what?

*(No one has an answer.)*

LACKEY: Any last words?

JOSH *(nodding, as soon as he can draw a breath):* God forgive you . . . you don't know what you're doing.

LACKEY: You people make me so sick.

*(He flashes out a stiletto and plunges it into* JOSH's *side.* JOSH *and* SIMON *cry out, fall.* LACKEY *and* HENCHMAN *leave, looking to see if their escape is observed. No one interferes. All lights fade to black and stay that way for a long time.)*

# Scene Thirteen

*(Lights come up very slowly on the area surrounding the "lake."* ANDREW *and* JIM *enter, nearing the end of a long debate.)*

JIM: No, I mean it. His ideas were sound, I mean they had the ring of truth about them . . . I guess he just couldn't follow through with them.

ANDREW: But he knew he was going to die. He knew it.

JIM: Well, he had reached a kind of point of no return.

ANDREW: Better for all of us just to lie low for a while.

JIM: I don't know what to do. *(The lit area expands to include the "lake" with the boat, and in the boat is a very somber* SIMON.*)*

JIM: Hi, Peter.

ANDREW: Brother. (SIMON *does not even seem to notice them, but he poles the boat close to them so they can step in. He is like a man in a trance.)* Any fish today?

*(No reply. Then finally he speaks.)*

SIMON: He seemed so sure. He really acted like he knew what he was doing. I believed him.

ANDREW: We all did, Peter.

SIMON: And in a way, I . . . I still do. Maybe I just can't accept that he's dead, but I feel . . . that's not all there is.

*(*JOSH *approaches, wearing a jacket with a hood that almost obscures his face. He approaches the boat and stands, watching. Pause.)*

JOSH: So. How're the fish biting?

SIMON *(shrugs):* Ah, you know. (JOSH *turns and walks away.* SIMON *realizes who he is and is electrified.)* How are the fish biting! *(He stands straight up in the boat, almost tossing* JIM *and* ANDREW *into the water.)* It's him . . . I knew it! It is him! *(He starts to pole the boat back to shore.)*

JIM: Peter, don't be ridiculous . . .

SIMON: It's him.

ANDREW *(to* JIM*):* He's been out here in the sun all day.

JIM: Hey, Peter, why don't you just get out of the boat and walk across the water to him?

SIMON: Shut up! It's really him!

*(He climbs out of the boat and runs to* JOSH, *who folds back the hood to show his face. It is, of course, really him.* SIMON *holds out his arms to embrace him, but* JOSH *stops him with a gesture: three fingers.* SIMON *staggers, falls back. The lights on the "lake" dim out.* JOSH *and* SIMON *are alone.)*

SIMON: I know. I'm sorry. I am so sorry. I denied you three times! But do you know what I've been through since . . . since then? I died when they killed you.

JOSH: Yes. I know. You've been through the furnace, the dry heat that turns soft clay . . . into stone. That fuses sand . . . into a rock. It can even make a rock where once there was only a clumsy, bigmouthed fisherman from nowhere. (SIMON *dares to look up at* JOSH's *face.* JOSH *holds the three fingers in front of* SIMON's *face.*)

JOSH: Peter. Do you love me?

SIMON *(confused):* Well . . . of course I do, what . . . ?

JOSH: Feed my lambs.

SIMON: Sure. Lambs, OK. (JOSH *closes his fist, holds up only two fingers.*) But . . .

JOSH: Peter. Do you really love me?

SIMON: How can you ask that? After all we've been through together . . .

JOSH: Then tend my sheep.

SIMON: Well, sure, I . . .

(JOSH *closes his fist, holds up only one finger.* SIMON *stares at it; he is beginning to understand.*)

SIMON: Sheep . . . right!

JOSH: Peter. This is important. Do you love me?

SIMON: You know everything. So you know that I do.

JOSH: I do. I know that you gave up everything you had to follow me. You've done very, very well, despite what you or anybody else says. Now . . . feed my sheep.

SIMON: I will. I will! (JOSH *shows no fingers.*) That's it? You mean . . . ?

(JOSH *reaches up with the fist to rap on* SIMON's *forehead, but* SIMON *stops him and raps on his own forehead with his own fist. They smile.*)

SIMON: How can you still want me, after all the stupid things I've done?

JOSH: Peter, you've got to understand something. It's one of the things I want you to tell people about me.

SIMON: OK . . .

JOSH: It's this. I'm not interested in who people *used* to be. I'm interested in who they are *capable of becoming.*

SIMON: So . . . to you, I'm . . . I'm . . .

JOSH *(grinning):* Say it!

SIMON: The Rock?

JOSH: That's right. Now . . . you'll find that where I'm sending you will be difficult, a hard place to work.

SIMON: Where's that?

JOSH: Everywhere. To everybody. With you on the one hand and the whole world on the other, everybody's going to be, uh, between a rock and a hard place. It gives us a fighting chance, at least. Irresistible force finally meets immovable object: you.

(JOSH *pats him on the shoulder and turns away.*)

SIMON: Where are you going?

JOSH: Away.

SIMON: I want to go with you.

JOSH: You will. Don't rush it. Meanwhile, I'll be with you. Always. Up to, and including, the end of the world.

(*He goes.* SIMON *watches him go. Once* JOSH *is gone,* SIMON *turns to his brothers, and the light comes back up to show them staring at him.*)

SIMON: Well? Come on!

(*They stare at him.*)

JIM: Come on where?

SIMON: *We're going fishing!*

(*The lights dim. They are cross-fading into the next scene.*)


# Scene Fourteen


(*Another area of the stage is lighting up to show the other followers:* MADELINE, MARY, JOHN, THEO. *Into this circle comes* SIMON, *who talks with them in elaborate mime; the entire sequence that follows is mimetic: various areas of the stage light up and then darken, with* SIMON *running in and out of them with appropriate actions. The music is fast, energetic.*

(*In vignettes that follow, we see* SIMON *healing the crippled, preaching with great authority, being imprisoned, and being embraced by his new "brothers and sisters" wherever he goes. Finally we see him raise a little girl from the dead! And for our benefit he raises triumphant fists over his head, like a champion boxer. He is Rocky; he is the Rock.*

(*His light fades slowly.*

(*Then the lights rise to show a private meeting of believers. All of the disciples are there except* JUDITH. *Into this come* LACKEY *and* HENCHMAN, *bearing their usual weapons. All assembled shout disapproval: "What are you doing here?" and so on.*)

LACKEY: We hate to interrupt such a lovely gathering.

HENCHMAN: But we got our orders, same as anybody else.

SIMON: What do you want?

LACKEY: Boss wants to talk with you.

HENCHMAN: Just for a minute.

*(All shout objections.)*

SIMON: I understand.

*(More objections)*

THEO: Peter, don't! Those guys are . . . they'll *kill* you.

SIMON: I told the Teacher I wanted to follow him wherever he went. This is the only place he went that I haven't been. It's OK.

*(LACKEY and HENCHMAN lead him away. As they near the exit;)*

THEO: Peter?

*(He looks back. THEO makes a strong positive gesture, some sort of "right on" sign. SIMON smiles, returns it, then goes. There is a moment as the remaining believers watch the place where they last saw their inspired leader. Slowly the scene lights fade down to black, but the music continues—the play is not over.)*

# Scene Fifteen

*(The lighting that we saw at the very beginning of the play restores. TEACHER and TWO sit, looking at the book.)*

TWO: Wow. What a great story, man! I never dreamed. Are there any more like that?

TEACHER *(laughs):* Oh, yes. In fact . . . well, I guess if they had written down every single thing that happened . . . the whole world couldn't hold all the books.

TWO: Wow.

TEACHER: So I figure, hey, learn all you can about the ones we *do* have. *(A beat, then)* I gotta go. See you soon.

*(TWO sits, enthralled with the book. He turns the pages, looking for another story to read.)*

*(In another area of the stage, the kids we have seen playing "scissors-paper-stone" appear once more. This time they are calling the combinations out loud):*

PLAYER ONE: Scissors. Rock. Rock breaks scissors.

PLAYER TWO: Paper. Rock. Paper wraps rock.

PLAYER ONE: Paper. Scissors. Scissors cut paper.

*(They both come up with "stone.")*

PLAYER TWO: Rock.

*(They try again—same result.)*

PLAYER ONE: Rock.

*(And again. They pause. They look at each other . . .)*

BOTH: Rock!

*(Their light fades to black. TWO is alone in a spot. He looks up from his reading, inspired. The spot narrows to blackout.)*

## THE END

# APPENDIX A

## INSTRUCTIONS FOR FOLDING
## THE ORIGAMI DOVE

Start with a square—8" x 8" for example

Fold it in half—

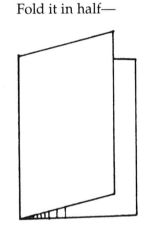

now cut a triangle out of the corner like this:

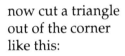

Now you have the paper that Madeline gives Josh.

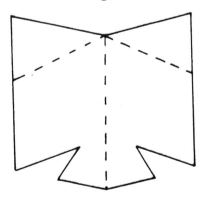

Fold the corners toward the middle like this:

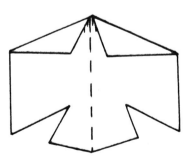

Then fold it in half as before. It should look like this so far:

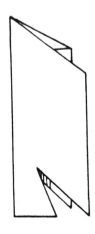

Fold the HEAD one way—

then back the other way, along the same crease.

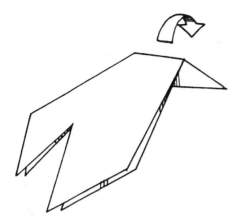 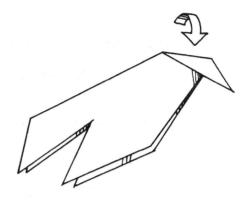

Now you can push the head DOWN along its CENTER CREASE

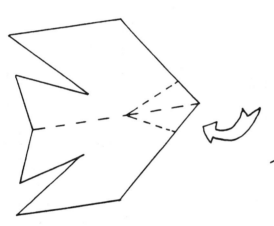 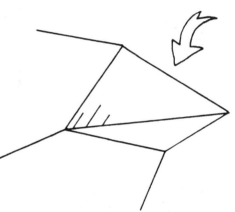

so that it looks like this:

Fold up the wings, and VOILA!

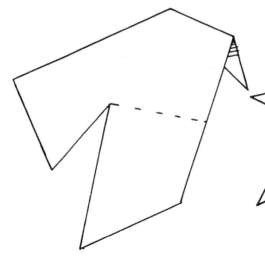 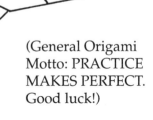

(General Origami Motto: PRACTICE MAKES PERFECT. Good luck!)

# APPENDIX B

## SUGGESTED STAGE FLOOR PLAN

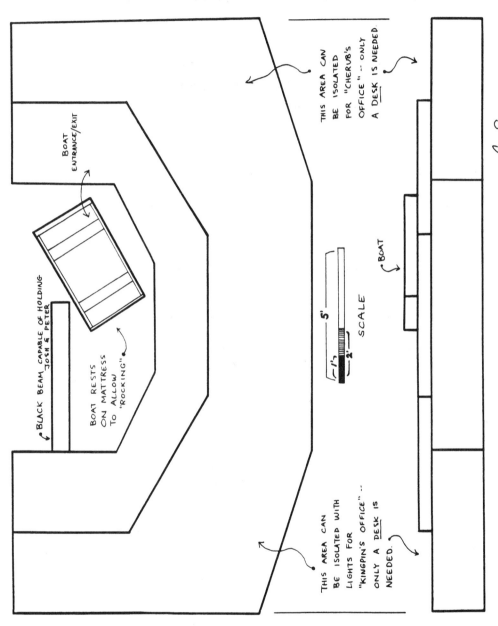

# PERFORMANCE LICENSING AGREEMENT

**Lillenas Drama Resources**
**Performance Licensing**
P.O. Box 419527, Kansas City, MO 64141

Name _____

Organization _____

Address _____

City _____ State _____ ZIP _____

Play _____

Number of performances intended _____

Approximate dates _____

Amount remitted* $_____

Mail to Lillenas at the address above

Order performance copies of this script from your local bookstore or directly from the publisher.

*$25.00 for the first performance; $15.00 each subsequent performance.